NEW BLACK CYCLONES

NEW BLACK CYCLONES

Racism, Representation and Revolutions of
Power in Cycling

MARLON LEE MONCRIEFFE

BLOOMSBURY SPORT
LONDON • OXFORD • NEW YORK • NEW DELHI • SYDNEY

BLOOMSBURY SPORT
Bloomsbury Publishing Plc
50 Bedford Square, London, WC1B 3DP, UK
29 Earlsfort Terrace, Dublin 2, Ireland

BLOOMSBURY, BLOOMSBURY SPORT and the Diana logo are trademarks of Bloomsbury
Publishing Plc

First published in Great Britain 2024

A catalogue record for this book is available from the British Library

Library of Congress Cataloguing-in-Publication data has been applied for

ISBN: HB: 978-1-3994-0556-0; eBook: 978-1-3994-0561-4; ePdf: 978-1-3994-0558-4

2 4 6 8 10 9 7 5 3 1

Illustrations on pp. 1, 21, 43, 55, 74, 84, 104, 110, 120, 145, 173 by Angelo Mutangana. Images on
pp. viii, 38, 63, 70, 78, 82, 90, 92 by Getty Images. Images on pp. v and 163 by Shutterstock. Other
images are author's own or as credited.

Front cover images all by Getty Images. From left to right, top to bottom: Daniel Teklehaimanot,
Teniel Campbell, Llori Sharpe, Nicholas Dlamini, Biniam Girmay.

Back cover. Left to right, credit in brackets. Red Walters (Red Walters), Maize Wimbush
(Bahati Foundation), Henok Mulubrhan (FERWACY Tour du Rwanda), Nicholas Paul (Getty),
Taky Marie-Divine Kouamé (Getty)

Typeset in Minion Pro by Deanta Global Publishing Services, Chennai, India
Printed and bound in Great Britain by CPI Group (UK) Ltd., Croydon, CR0 4YY

To find out more about our authors and books visit www.bloomsbury.com
and sign up for our newsletters

CONTENTS

INTRODUCTION

In November 2021, a 'New Black Cyclone' appeared to storm across the world's cycling scene. The incredible Biniam Girmay of Eritrea produced a mighty, explosive sprint to finish ahead of the chasing peloton in the Under-23 UCI World Championships road race in the Flanders region of Belgium. In claiming a silver medal, he became known as 'the first Black' cyclist to stand on the podium in the event. I saw how the cycling media were instantly enthralled by the emergence of this young and gifted cycling athlete from Africa. It seemed that it would only be a short matter of time before Girmay would storm again.

He did, with a sprint finish victory, again in Flanders, at the Gent-Wevelgem classic race, on 27 March 2022. From this, the cycling media began an influential discourse, stating that 'history' was being made right before our eyes, through a ground-breaking moment in the sport:

'Biniam Girmay: Eritrean becomes first African to win a one-day classic with Gent-Wevelgem victory.' – *BBC Sport*

'Cycling history was written on a sunny Sunday afternoon in Wevelgem, Belgium when 21-year-old Eritrean rider Biniam Girmay (Intermarché–Wanty–Goubert Matériaux) became the first African rider to win a classic.' – *Velo*

Girmay continued with momentum and force. He followed his Gent-Wevelgem victory with what was described as a 'historic' 'first Black African' victory on stage 10 of the 2022 Giro d'Italia. At the Tour de France in 2024, Girmay produced a sensational sprint victory on stage 3 of the race. 'The first Black', 'the first Black African' and 'First Black Man in History to Win a Tour de France Stage' were some of the cycling media headline terms used to announce his feat. Girmay stormed again. He won stages 8 and 13 for a hat-trick of victories. He wore the green jersey throughout most of the race to denote his leadership of the sprinters' competition. He sealed overall triumph at the tour's conclusion in Nice, where he was crowned as the best sprinter in the world's most renowned cycling race. What a champion!

The cycling media boom in attention towards Girmay, and the racial emphasis on him being 'the first Black' rider to achieve success, was, in my view, framed in a similar way to the emergence and breakthrough successes of the original cycling media-named 'Black Cyclone' – the track sprint sensation, Marshall 'Major' Taylor (1878–1932) of the USA. Early on in his professional racing career, as a Black cycling athlete, he stormed on to a white-dominated cycling scene.

I also saw similarities in 'first Black' language of Girmay's representation, in what I had shared in my 2021 book, *Desire, Discrimination, Determination – Black Champions in Cycling* – a historical and contemporary narrative biographical account on the experiences of aspirant, elite and professional Black cycling athletes, who over the years had competed in white-dominated spaces. In my accounts, I illuminated the peculiar and complex oxymoronic existence of the solitary Black cycling athlete. These individuals have sometimes been revered as the 'extraordinary' being, while at other times they have been looked upon, by the same dominant white gaze, as the freak 'novelty', existing as the 'other' or as a possible threat to the status quo of these exclusively white cycling spaces.

This book, *New Black Cyclones*, takes my explorations of racism, and the representation of Black people in the sport of cycling, much further than before.

I present on and critique historical and contemporary examples of white sanction in cycling – an exclusive endorsement given to Black people from the white people who hold the power of enablement for allowing access and possible advancement in the sport. I share my reflections on Black people's views and experiences in the sport by giving a portrayal of cycling since the Black Lives Matter anti-racism protests across the world in 2020. I focus on incidents of racism, and I explore where anti-racism protest and activism has aimed to challenge this, for changing the way in which the sport can be better represented.

I present accounts of my journeys across the USA, where I visited Black cyclists of grassroots communities in New York City; Philadelphia, Pennsylvania; Charlotte, North Carolina, and Atlanta, Georgia. I share my learning from engaging with their cycling cultures, in witnessing the self-empowerment of Black people together as 'New Black Cyclones', transforming how the sport is seen.

In 2025 the UCI World Championship road racing events are set to take place in Rwanda, central-eastern Africa. This has provided me with thought to the immediate, and long-term possibilities on the way in which the sport could be viewed as genuinely advancing to become more globally inclusive and equitable in its representation. Still, given this 'interest-convergence' of Europe moving towards embracing Africa and African people, I ask questions: Is this shift of interest towards Africa simply a new phase of European colonialism, repeating itself as cycling's 'scramble for Africa', for seizing control of Africa's untapped potential in cycling?* What do Black cyclists from Africa predict will happen for the representation of cycling during the 2025 UCI World Championship road races, and after this event?

I wanted to understand the extent to which the powerful and authoritative communication and representation of cycling as a sport

* Interest-convergence: Derrick Bell, the late African American legal scholar conceived this term to explain how Black people may only be given the sense of progress with racial equality if their cause converges with the self-interests of powerful white people.

given by the European imagination has an influence on Black people in cycling to believe, think and do by this frame of reference. I aimed to see how Black people in self-empowerment and self-determination were developing their own cycling utopias across their Western nations and across the African continent

I travelled widely across Africa, to meet with Black people involved with leading the sport of cycling in central-eastern Africa – Kigali, Rwanda. I travelled to South Africa to Cape Town, Johannesburg, Soweto and Bethlehem to meet Black leaders in cycling, to learn from them. I travelled to Western Africa, to the city of Freetown, Sierra Leone, and to the city of Accra, Ghana, to meet Black leaders of the sport, and further to the rural Ghanian Peki Volta region for more learning.

Through my journeys across the cycling cultures of Black people, from Africa, and those Black people of the African diaspora, in the USA and in the UK, I aimed to make sense of any common patterns of shared experiences, through their responses to the questions of my curiosity. By my sharing of their testimonies in this book, I want to champion their thoughts, and their voices, shifting these from the often unheard, and unrecognised margins of the sport, to a more central positioning of value.

1

How far can the bicycle take you?

It was the morning of the inaugural Freetown Criterium Classic in Sierra Leone, held in November 2023. My cycling team – Team Ubuntu – and I had planned carefully for this. I created this team earlier in the year, and I'd travelled over from the UK to provide my riders with some support and coaching advice. We'd got in some good training miles; long rides along the Freetown Peninsula to Bureh Beach and back. We'd ridden around the loop of the race course, figuring out where the possible breaks could come. We'd practised our sprint efforts multiple times, starting 500 metres out from the finish line. We'd been riding every day for an entire week, but there was one thing we hadn't organised; that I hadn't thought of. We needed a motorbike to follow the race to support the team with spare wheels and water.

I had suggested to Fatima (Deborah) Conteh, Team Ubuntu's road captain, that she find a boy from her community to help us, and we'd pay him to sit on the back of a motorcycle – if we could find a motorcyclist – but I'd woken to a stream of WhatsApp messages from her:

'The boy is here with me. . .'

'Can't find motorbike. . .'

'Race will start soon.'

In the oppressive heat I'd been guzzling litres of water, Coca-Cola, Fanta and Sprite all week during our training rides, so I knew we definitely needed the motorbike and the boy to carry the fluids. 'I will come now and will find a motorbike,' I responded, but I had no idea how I would make that happen.

I rushed downstairs to grab a speedy breakfast and bumped into the hotel manager. He was a Sierra Leonean man, but he'd told me that he'd lived in East London for a good few years and sounded like the *Luther* actor, Idris Elba.

'Good morning! Are you all set for today? And the team?' he enquired.

I'd previously told him that this was my first time in Sierra Leone and that I was here to support my cycling team.

'Good morning! I've just got to get myself over to the start line, as soon as I can. It's near the Cotton Tree Junction. We actually need to get a motorbike to help out with water and wheels, you know, to follow the race.'

'I might be able to help you,' he said.

'Really? Could you?' I responded.

'Yep. I have a few contacts who I can contact, right now.'

He held up his mobile phone. 'Leave it with me. I'll come back to you,' he said, as he walked away to make enquiries. He seemed serious enough. I didn't really know.

I was looking out for him, but I didn't see him, so I finished my breakfast and was just about to leave for the Cotton Tree Junction when he reappeared. 'Hi! I've sorted it. Cyrille, my head of security, rides a motorbike. You can have him for the day, free of charge. He's putting his boots on, right now.'

This seemed like a gift, and I was extremely grateful, not to mention relieved, and Cyrille seemed very pleased to be part of the team, too. I jumped on the back of his motorbike to take a short journey of around 15 minutes from the hotel, past the finish line of the race on Beach Road in the Aberdeen area of Freetown, and towards the city centre. It was a smooth journey. I jumped off the motorbike and walked through the crowd of riders and supporters, searching for my team, and found them at the very back of the field, in their distinctive pink Team Ubuntu jerseys, looking pretty anxious.

I introduced Cyrille and the young boy took the spare wheels and cooler box from Deborah.

'There is the motorbike. Go and get ready with him,' she instructed, and the pair went off to get in position. I stood back to let Deborah focus on the race with our Team Ubuntu riders, Esther Mansaray and Blessing Jabbie.

'Good luck! Be safe. I'll see you on the finishing line!' I said, even though I wanted to tell them to go and line up at the front of what must have been around 80 riders, but we were here, we'd made it on time, and so I left it. Moments later, the race was waved away. Riders, motorcyclists and an ambulance, all at once, moving together through the denser city streets.

The Freetown Criterium Classic race was the idea of the Flames Cycling Club of Freetown, Sierra Leone. They wanted to promote bicycle racing in the capital city of their country, where the sport had rarely occurred before. So, they had organised this race, and all of the teams from across Sierra Leone including Lunsar Cycling Team, Kono Cycling Team, C2C Primus, Lungi and Makeni, had brought their best men, junior men and women's teams to compete in this, the inaugural event.

Although this event was dubbed a criterium, the race course did not really represent this. A criterium is normally raced around a circuit of between roughly 800 metres to 1.5 kilometres, however this race would have the cyclists ride from Cotton Tree Junction for around 15 kilometres heading south through the city towards the Peninsula highway. For the women's race, around 5 kilometres after reaching the Lumley Beach interchange, they would make a U-turn and then race back towards the

Beach Road area, heading for Aberdeen, a coastal neighbourhood in the northwestern part of the capital. From here, the women would race for four laps of a 7km circuit race route including the long straights of Aberdeen Road and Wilkinson Road to a finish line at the end of the Beach Road in Aberdeen, very near to the hotel in which I was staying. The men's and the junior race was a longer test. This would carry on for another 10 kilometres or so past the Lumley Beach interchange before returning to race the 7km circuit, six of these for the men and four for the junior men. Although all the riders started together in Cotton Tree, it was assumed that a split in the field between the men, junior men and women riders would happen.

What next? I had to get back to Aberdeen to be close to the finish line. I looked around, and noticed one motorcycle taxi rider. I considered it for a moment. Then, walking towards him, I called over, 'Can you follow the race for me?'

'Yes. Get on,' he responded. 'Follow the race? I don't know the route.'

'What? You don't know the route? Are you sure? OK. Ride towards Lumley Beach. I know this is the way, and as soon as we pick up a cyclist, we can take it from there.'

We set off – and I immediately realised I was in for one helluva motorbike ride. Every near accident we encountered – and there were plenty – would prompt abusive expletives from my driver and one-handed gestures at the cars, other motorbikes and motorised rickshaw taxis, known locally as kek-keks, that feature prominently on the Freetown streets. People frequently pull out without looking and, although the motorbike taxi drivers wear helmets, their passengers don't. I wondered how it was for my cyclists, having to race in the chaos of it all. We sped on and I began to see some of the backmarkers from the women's race. First one, then another, then another and then – oh no! – I realised it was Esther, one of our stronger riders. She'd been dropped and was riding solo through the traffic.

'Keep going!' I urged the motorcycle taxi driver. I was looking for Blessing, as this was her first ever bike race. She had been nervous about it all week. I didn't see her, so I suspected she might have pulled out. We passed more female riders who had fallen out of the back, more cars and more kek-keks, until I eventually caught sight of a pink Team Ubuntu jersey at the head of the race with a few other riders. We rode up to see Deborah working hard, the front of her jersey fully unzipped, now more like a cape in the wind, she was sweating it out and hurting. Cyrille and the boy on their motorbike were also there, so now we had one rider plus two motorbikes at the front of the race – two more than any other team, it seemed.

We followed to the Lumley Beach interchange and then a U-turn on to Beach Road and towards Aberdeen to start the circuits. After a couple of these, I told the motorcyclist to stop by the finish area. I had escaped serious injury and near death on the crowded streets of Freetown with this guy, and I paid him well, happy to climb off in one piece. I was familiar with the race finish area, and I had been here more than once during the week with the team for our sprint sessions. Today there was a party atmosphere. Reggae music was blasting, and spectators were out in numbers. I retreated from the hot sun to the peace of an empty restaurant by the finish line.

After a while, the men's peloton approached and flashed through, with the front of the women's race inside it. Four of them, including Deborah, had tagged on. This meant it would be just one more lap for the women in their race. Then some backmarkers of the men's race rode by, followed by an ambulance with sirens blasting. It pulled up and parked just over the finish line. The medics rushed out to open the rear doors and attend to a male rider, lying on a stretcher with what seemed to me to be dehydration. There was a small crowd. Eventually, the rider got up and walked away with his friends, but the ambulance didn't move. I wondered whether a vehicle that was here for the safety of the riders was actually causing a dangerous hazard by parking there, but then again perhaps not as many other vehicles were also parked next to the finish line.

It seemed like only a short time had passed, but the front of the men's race flashed through once again to the vibrant yells of spectators and motorbike horns sounding. I didn't see any female racers with them this time around. They'd be coming in for their own finish, it seemed. Beneath the beating reggae music booming from the speakers there was a low hum of anticipation. Spectators began to gather at the finish line and some photographers with their huge cameras were taking up their positions. 'This be must it!' I thought. Jumping up, I left the restaurant. I got out my mobile phone, ready to record the climax, and there she was. Deborah was at the front with another rider in pursuit, over the speed bumps, into the last 200 metres, just as we'd practised. The spectators were screaming. Deborah was out of the saddle, legs pumping. Then sat back down with arms and head aloft to the sky, expression ecstatic. Cyrille followed, tooting his motorbike horn madly in celebration, the boy behind him with his arms in the air. Deborah had won the Freetown Criterium Classic and achieved a wonderful maiden victory for Team Ubuntu.

'How far can the bicycle take you?' This had become my opening question to audiences on my book tour across the UK, Europe, USA and South Africa, sharing stories from my book, *Desire, Discrimination, Determination* (2021). I would not have been in Sierra Leone for the Freetown Criterium Classic without the momentum created by the journey I took with that book. And I would not have written that book if I had not got into the sport and become a racer back in 1994 with the Redmon Cycling Club of Morden, southwest London, so for me personally, the bicycle had taken me quite a long way.

My Sunday morning club rides became regular from my home on the Alton Estate of Roehampton, London, to the club ride meeting place in Sutton, then out on to the North Downs of Surrey, to places that seemed far away: Box Hill, Ranmore Common, Leith Hill and Whitedown, and sometimes over to the West Sussex Downs of Bury Hill, Slindon Common, Goodwood, Duncton, Amberley and Pulborough. The summer-time Tuesday evening burn-ups through Roehampton Gate in to Richmond Park for multiple laps and the Thursday evening 10-mile time trials bombing up and down the dual carriageway from Dorking to Holmwood and back all gave me the speed and conditioning required in becoming a bike racer.

I didn't get into cycling dreaming of representing my country at the Olympic Games or riding in the Tour de France. Not at all. I didn't live next door to a velodrome or a BMX track, cycling was not something that I did at school as part of the PE curriculum, and neither was it habitual for anyone in my family. I left school at 16 and it was a few years later that I decided I would begin to ride my bike among the cars, buses, trucks and motorcycles to work from Roehampton, across southwest London to Bermondsey, southeast London, a 20-mile round trip. I rode every day, and always fast and on the limit, because in my mind that was the only way and what the bike was for. I rode in every season, in sunshine, wind, rain, snow and sleet. Nothing stopped me. I raced against other people; familiar faces I would see on their bikes, on their motorbikes, in their cars just to prove that I could get from A to B quicker than them. I'd repeat all of this on the way home as well.

It was in the summer of 1994; I got talking to a friend at work named Mick Deen. Mick was a white man, and much older than me. I'd come across him regularly on his bike during the morning commute and we would often end up racing with each other for fun. He told me he was a bike racer, and he invited me to do a time trial with him. I refused, I didn't want to know, but he kept bugging me about it, so eventually I did, and that's how I got into it. I would do the time trials whenever I was able to hitch a lift from Mick to an event, or if necessary, by taking the train out of London to the Surrey Hills and Sussex Downs. I became the club champion for the 10 miles time trial in August 1998. But I was in and out of the sport, cash was low, as I'd left full-time work by that time to undertake university studies. To earn some money, I took a job as a London bicycle courier. I was riding around 50 or 60 miles a day across London. I was paid for the amount of deliveries I made in a day, and I would beat the motorbike couriers to the jobs. I won the hill-climb championships in 1999, and then when I started to get into road racing, I won a string of those races in 2000 and received the club's champion rider trophy for this too. All of this made me feel proud. But I didn't completely buy into the racing, it wasn't as if it was a sport for making a good living like the millions of pounds that could be made for being a footballer. Racing was just a hobby and for the love of fitness. So, I took some years out of racing to focus on qualifying to become a primary school teacher, but I didn't stop riding my bike.

Paul Wright

I'm pictured here racing in a time-trial in Surrey, England, 2006

I returned to racing in 2004 for time trialling, and road racing, and I began to get involved in track racing too. In 2005, I joined Agiskoviner cycling team. This brought together some of the best London and South East-based elite riders. At this point, I was able to travel to races around the country more independently. I'd competed in a few races or had been at the same events with an older, but still on fire, Russell Williams and a younger, and very powerful, Christian Lyte. Williams won 18 British cycling national championships for road and track racing between 1976 and 2002. Lyte won three World junior track sprint titles when representing Great Britain between 2006 and 2007. They both stood out to me for their intelligent racing skills, but also because both were clearly of mixed-ethnic heritage. I later learned they both had African-Caribbean and English ethnic group heritage. I had also heard about another rider of similar mixed-ethnic heritage called Maurice Burton who'd won three national titles for track cycling between 1973 and 1975, and there was a road racer called Mark McKay, whom I knew about because I had seen his name in the cycling media for some of his national circuit series wins. However, apart from these guys there wasn't really anyone else that I knew of who looked like them, or looked like me, with a darker skin tone and both parents of African-Caribbean ethnic group heritage, in the sport.

I remained generally unconscious of the dearth of Black people on the UK cycling scene and what the reasons for that could be, but this changed in 2009 when I came across a thread discussion on a cycling website called Time trialling Forum. I'd normally check into this online forum simply to find out about start sheet entries of races and results, and the website appeared to be run by an administrative group of club riders. They opened a discussion entitled 'Whites only' with the words:

'Time trialling has always been a mainly male sport – the figures show it; but throughout my 45 years of involvement with the pastime, it has always been a virtually 100% white sport. Yes, I know we can always quote "What about so-and-so who used to be in the whatsit wheelers" – but generally, our scene does not appeal to our ethnic brethren, and you very rarely see a rider with anything more than a suntan. Any thoughts as to why?'

What seemed to be an informal enquiry out of curiosity caused a wave of dumb responses, like this one:

'Firstly, I wonder if the physiological differences of Black and Asian people in comparison with Caucasian has any bearing? Apart from Major Taylor from around 100 years ago and a handful of Black and Asian sprinters (the 84 Olympic sprint champ) I can't think of a single world class Black or Asian road rider.'

This respondent means Nelson Vails of the USA, who won the silver medal in the 1984 Olympic sprint, but it is also a shame that this respondent didn't know that Grégory Baugé of France became the UCI World Track Sprint Champion in 2009. The ignorant pseudo-scientific racist assumptions continue:

'This situation exists in swimming and is apparently due to average leg length as proportion of total height being longer and thus the smaller torso causes less buoyancy. Perhaps in cycling there's an issue here that causes a lower than the (average) Caucasian power to weight ratio rendering endurance cycling a more difficult sport in which to be competitive with Caucasians.'

This kind of talk by white people about the absence of Black people in cycling, on a public forum, was an example to me of the ignorant white gaze being trained on Black people – although these are just a couple of examples and I'm not generalising about all white people in cycling or society as a whole, just the speculative idiots in general.

Following some good times, bad times and better times in my time trialling, and some horrible losses and wonderful road-racing victories, I eventually committed to track sprinting. I mixed my racing with my day job as a teacher, and I lived nowhere near a velodrome, so all my training was on the turbo trainer and on drag strip (dead straight downhill roads). I was competing with some of the best riders in the country in the National Sprinters League, National Grass Track Sprint events, British Cycling National Championships, UEC European and UCI World Championships in the UK and across Europe. My racing took me to places I would never have thought of before – from Yorkshire to Lincolnshire to Suffolk in England for Grass track sprint racing, to Eastern Europe and Minsk in Belarus, to Bordeaux in France and Anadia in Portugal for track sprint velodrome racing.

Over the years a string of more good days than bad, and some nice wins along the way, resulted in an invitation to attend the British Cycling 50th Anniversary Awards Dinner in Manchester in 2010 to receive an award in acknowledgement of a UEC European medal win in the team sprint in 2009. This was a very special moment for me, being part of a celebration of the sport among some of its greatest and most influential leaders, and this was also the inaugural induction of cyclists to British Cycling's Hall of Fame. There was not one Black-British rider being inducted, but this was an area of change that I would lead on with British Cycling later down the line in 2021; more on this to follow.

During the years 2008 to 2013 as a primary school teacher, I was creating new school cycling teams and leading British Cycling's Go-Ride programme of cycling events for young people, their families and the local community. I was also encouraging children and their parents to enter the British Schools Cycling Association (BSCA) racing events that were being organised and held across the country. I volunteered to become the BSCA membership secretary for a short time. I led BSCA and their members in my hosting some of their Schools' National

Cycling Championships. Being involved with BSCA as a leader, teacher and parent also gave me the opportunity to travel around the country for cycling competitions, visiting lots of Yorkshire towns and cities, and across the East and West Midlands too. All of this gave me a passage into different social environments and cycling cultures, and I saw the sport's various disciplines at the grassroots.

However, there was a total absence of Black parents and their children as riders in these cultures at this grassroots level. In fact, my young daughter and I were often the only Black people attending these Schools' National Cycling Championship events. She managed to win multiple national championship titles, and we met some really lovely cycling people, but we also met some who were uncomfortable with Black people. In September 2023 a film went viral on social media of a Black girl at a March 2022 gymnastics competition in Ireland being blatantly ignored at a medal ceremony.

A similar sort of incident happened to my daughter at a 2015 BSCA National Championship Roller Racing event in Rugeley, Staffordshire. A Roller Racing competition sees cyclists going head-to-head, sometimes up to four on them racing in sprint matches usually over two distances: 500 metres and 1 kilometre using bicycles fixed to the ground, and the support of a person as their holder. The bicycles are attached to computers that can register each rider's speed and progress against each other, and this information is displayed by projector on a screen behind the riders, each having a different coloured dial indicator measuring their progress so that the audience can watch and cheer along. We'd prepared well for the championships. She beat all the girls and even all of the boys in her age group. But, at the end of the racing for everyone, when it came to calling her up for her win, the organisers skipped this. I remember how my daughter and I looked at each other in confusion, wondering what was going on. But the organisers continued on with other age group awards until the end of the ceremony. Then they began to wind up the event with thanks and goodbyes, and I remember some people were looking over at me and my daughter and at the event organisers and wondering what was going on too. They eventually called the girls up for their medals. The correct national bronze and silver medals were awarded to the riders, but when my daughter came

11

back to me, I saw that they had given her an inferior tiny-looking medal that was not from the national competition. There was no way I was going to let them get away with that. I went up on stage and quietly but firmly instructed them to present her with the national gold medal that she'd won. All of this left a stain on what is supposed to be a celebration of cycling for young people.

Another BSCA national championship event that we'd attended before this was the 2013 National Roller Racing Championships in Bradford, a city with a large British-Asian population, yet the competitors and parents were all white, apart from my daughter and me. The racing and medal ceremony were taking place in a local multi-sports centre, and we were in the gymnastics hall. Above it were public viewing galleries, and I can remember looking up to see lots of curious British-Asian people stopping what they were doing to observe, staring at us from the galleries for long periods of time. Here was the world of cycling, perhaps totally unfamiliar and framed as an inaccessible space to them. They would not have seen anybody looking like them, at that time, and less than one year after the 2012 Olympic Games in London, the communication of cycling was being amplified by the media in its representation of white British cycling heroes.

As a Black man I have entered a broad range of white-peopled spaces in cycling over the years in my multiple identities as a racer, teacher, parent and academic. This has given me clear evidence of how white people dominate the control and influence of the sport. From what I have seen, white people own, lead and manage cycling spaces, businesses, resources and finance, which means white people control cycling culture, and the narratives and histories that we hear and learn about. This brings me to sharing the rationale for my original enquiry into the dominance of whiteness in British cycling through my 'Made in Britain: Uncovering the life-histories of Black-British Champions in Cycling' project. I conceived this project with a view to creating and disseminating an original, subversive and alternative narrative of British cycling through the collective lives and voices of Black-British people. This project would take me to new paths of revelation on my cycling journey.

In 2015, the sport of cycling in Britain was described by *Cycling Weekly* as being in a 'golden age'. This sense and feeling had come from the momentum generated by gold medal successes at the 2004 Olympic

Games in Athens; in Beijing in 2008; the UCI Road World Championship victory for Mark Cavendish in 2011; followed by multiple gold medal successes for Great Britain's cyclists at the 2012 London Olympic Games, and before this, arguably the zeitgeist being Sir Bradley Wiggins' superb Tour de France victory in July 2012. All of this triggered a tsunami of hype and this enormous wave of interest, never seen before, led to a plethora of national honours being bestowed on the country's celebrated cyclists. They received knighthoods, damehoods, and CBE, OBE and MBE medals galore. From being a fairly minor sport that arguably ranked much lower in the public consciousness than, say, football, cricket or rugby union, the emergence of these cycling superstars transformed the sport, which became a source of British national pride.

I saw clearly how Britain's global cycling successes became a framework for fresh media communications of celebratory and triumphant white British historical representations, and how the popular appeal of white British cyclists saw them elevated by the media as cultural and historical icons of white British identity and white Britain's idealised past. The most common representation of Sir Bradley Wiggins saw him fitted frequently in quintessentially English Crombie woven suits and wearing long facial sideburns associated with Mod subculture of the late 1950s and 1960s. The media lionising of Wiggins fronting this public image is tied to a nostalgic golden age of white Britain's past – the Swinging Sixties. Here, the interconnection of a cycling superstar with cultural nostalgia appeals to white British familiarities and norms. The Mod is of popular appeal to both older and relatively current generations of the white British people through the identity of musicians in popular white British rock bands such as The Who in the 1960s; and later on, The Jam in the 1980s and Oasis during the 1990s/2000s. The extrinsic meaning given by the manufactured media and commercial representation of a cycling superstar, Sir Bradley Wiggins, in this way can also reveal underlying dominant white British majority group attitudes on what is most appealing and exclusively meaningful to them.

Another example of cultural exclusivity in the representation of white British cycling athletes was through London 2012 Olympic champion track sprinter Victoria Pendleton. She was marketed to the public as 'Britannia' – the female embodiment of Great Britain's

Empire and domination across the world, by its colonialism, land theft, the enslavement and genocide of people. All of this was incredible to see and passed without question. Pendleton was also promoted to the British public in a remake of Ridley Scott's Classic 1973 Hovis (English breadmaking company) television advert 'Boy on a Bike'. The original television advert was voted as Britain's favourite advert in a 2006 poll. Pendleton appeared on television screens dressed in traditional English costume as the girl on the bicycle making deliveries of brown bread while riding through the quintessential English thatched roof cottage village of Shaftesbury in Dorset. The constructed media and commercial representations of Sir Bradley Wiggins and Victoria Pendleton presented culturally nostalgic representations of the white British self, and in my view, this commercial use of white British cycling superstars reinforced a normative cultural ownership of cycling for white British people, engendering an invisible self-perpetuating sense of entitlement.

I wrote about this in *Velonews,* and in my book *Desire, Discrimination, Determination* in describing what I saw with track cycling at London 2012 as a 'Velodrome of whiteness'. The British Broadcasting Corporation (BBC) coverage of the 2012 Olympic Games seemed to be fully anchored from the London velodrome. It was a space where the nation could be drawn together and enthused by the triumphs of British cycling heroes and heroines. Members of the British establishment such as the Duke and Duchess of Cambridge were seen in attendance, anticipating victories for the nation. The vigorous waving of British union flags and the sea of white faces in the velodrome resembled the fervent nationalism displayed at the Royal Albert Hall in London at the 'Last Night of the Proms', an exclusive white British monocultural and monoethnic celebratory narrative of national identity. Similarly, Great Britain's all-white British track cycling team were presented in this way to the imagination of the nation, fuelled to glory by a partisan atmosphere of nationalism in the London velodrome.

The power generated in this space channelled and reinforced white British monocultural ethnic absolutism in nationalist identifications for how excellence in track cycling and its athletes is recognised and will be remembered as a norm. What was totally forgotten in that moment is that the 2012 London Olympic Games bid was won for Great Britain through an argument and promise that appealed to advancing a focus on London's unique racial and ethnic diversity; its everyday lived multiculturalism. The velodrome of whiteness contradicted the promise.

For me, I take an inclusive imagination of nation; I see the best of being British via the multicultural and multi-ethnic representation of its people, and this relates to my own multicultural upbringing and socialisation, being from London and in seeing Black and white people of Great Britain as gold medal winners at the 1980 Moscow and the 1984 Los Angeles Olympics: Daley Thompson, Seb Coe, Tessa Sanderson to name a few. So, as with all previous Olympic Games, I, too, wanted Olympic success for Great Britain and in London especially, the multicultural city where I was born, but as a Black-British man who had been involved in cycling in all its forms for over 20 years, and in seeing the national monocultural narrative of track cycling glory unfold, I had to ask – what about the Black-British cycling champions? They are there in track and field. They are there in football, and even in rugby. But never at the Olympics in road and track cycling. Where are the Black-British cycling road racers and track-racers? What are their stories?

By now I'd moved on from teaching in primary schools to become an academic. In 2016, as part of a life-history narratives conference at the University of Sussex, I shared with an academic audience a selection of images from the London velodrome of the 2012 Olympics – of Sir Bradley Wiggins as the cyclist 'mod rocker' of the Swinging Sixties, and the Olympic track cycling sprint champion Victoria Pendleton represented as Britannia – the female symbol of the British Empire. I put to my audience that these media images fuelled celebratory ethnocentric discourses through the raised profile given to the sport of cycling and its new heroes – basically the promotion of whiteness. My audience of white students and white academics were at first, I felt, pretty stunned by my presentation. Here was a Black academic examining the representation of white people in relation to Great Britain and racism in cycling, of all things. But as I encouraged the delegates to speak, they became more vocal in their criticism of the symbolic messages in the white British visual discourses of cycling.

It was there that I announced my research project, Made in Britain: Uncovering the life-histories of Black-British Champions in Cycling. I wanted to present a historic chronology of Black participation in cycling from grassroots level through amateur and up to professional level. I aimed to draw attention to Black-British champion cyclists through research and public engagement, and by sharing knowledge of their lives and successes in cycling. My aim was subversive in seeking to challenge the myopic presentation of white British cycling excellence in recent years. I was going to see how far the bicycle could take me in meeting with as many Black-British racing cyclists as possible – those who had either been national, European or World Champions and medallists at junior, senior or master levels in the sport, particularly in road and track cycling. I knew the riders were out there. Now was the time to collate their stories and to mix in some of my own story, to better understand my experiences in the sport, too. For those Black-British cyclists I would meet, I hoped they could use my study to reflect on their own racing careers and better understand some of their own experiences through the lives of similar others across their different generations.

The flyer for my 2018 research project

Over the next two years, I travelled to London, Manchester, the West Midlands and the East Midlands to meet with Black cyclists that I knew, such as Christian Lyte, Maurice Burton and Charlotte Cole-Hossain, the 2012 youth circuit race and 2017 junior track points race champion. I made contact with Russell Williams, who was living in Adelaide, Australia, and conversed with him online. I also met up with BMX riders too, including Tre Whyte, the 2014 UCI World Champion bronze medallist; Wayne Llewellyn, the European BMX champion in 1982, 1983 and 1984; and Charlie Reynolds, the British cruiser champion in 1985. He introduced me to Luli Adeyemo, the 1986 BMX World Champion, who was living in Sydney, Australia, so I made contact and spoke with her online. I created a network of knowledge through these Black-British cyclists that covered 50 years in the sport, and my conversations with them enabled me to capture critical testimonies from their lives in cycling and to start making meaning from their experiences.

From all of this, I curated a series of public exhibitions across the country to showcase the lives of Black-British cyclists through stories, photographs and memorabilia. These exhibitions occurred between December 2018 and October 2022, and were free to the general public. The first of these took place in Brighton in December 2018, and this attracted excellent national interest. Sir Bradley Wiggins began to follow the development of the project on my @BlackChampions_ Instagram page that some of my students (as my research assistants) had created for me. Wiggins seemed particularly interested in my presentation of Russell Williams's story, and he messaged me saying, 'He [Russell] was my role model as a young boy. A great man with a great heart. For me to be half the man he was when I grew up would have been enough.' This was a wonderful tribute. Williams was an influential cycling coach for Wiggins during his training days as a youth rider at the Herne Hill Velodrome in London. I responded by inviting Wiggins to lead a conversation with Williams, if I could bring him over to the UK from Australia for the second exhibition that I'd planned at the Herne Hill Velodrome in June 2019, and Wiggins accepted this invitation. He came along and met with me, and this turned into an inspirational reunion for a lot of people who were there, and particularly powerful I thought when the champion mentee – a white British cycling hero – openly praised and gave public recognition to the impact on his career from one of his early career mentors, a Black-British cycling champion.

Following the Herne Hill Velodrome event, the exhibition was presented to the general public in Leeds, Harrogate and Manchester in September 2019, Bristol in January 2022, Birmingham in June 2022, with the final exhibition in Guildford in October 2022. Some of the cyclists themselves attended the exhibitions in person and had conversations with the general public. The exhibitions changed many people's perceptions of contemporary bike racing culture. Where previously, people had only ever seen white faces, they were discovering new names that they had never heard of before. The visitors were also struck by these cyclists' desire and determination in overcoming implicit and explicit racial discrimination in cycling.

Here are some of the comments from members of the public who viewed the exhibitions held in Brighton, 2018, and at the Herne Hill Velodrome in 2019:

'I discovered new names that I had never heard of before I was here.'

'I didn't realise how many Black riders there were.'

'Fascinating exhibition telling an important story.'

'The personal stories have been excellent. Really illuminating. I think the combination of photos, objects and testimonies works really well. I now have a heightened awareness of Black achievement in cycling.'

'I didn't realise that there were so many brilliant Black cyclists.'

'I have been able to gain knowledge that I didn't know.'

'I wasn't aware of the under-representation of the Black cyclists' contribution to the sport.'

'Fascinating, heart-warming histories that demonstrate determination, grit and staying power.'

'Every one of them experienced discrimination. It's a massive shame on the sport.'

'This exhibition highlights a side to cycling I had never seen before. The determination to get to where they had; then for it to be taken away makes you question society.'

'Their dedication to their chosen sport. Their love of it despite the barriers they faced.'

'I feel angry for the lost opportunities for some of these great riders.'

An important aspect of the exhibitions in my public engagement campaign was to raise the profiles of Maurice Burton and Russell

Williams, as between them, they have won over 20 national cycling championship titles (Burton 3; Williams 18), so I was keen to persuade the national body for cycling, British Cycling, to induct both riders into the British Cycling Hall of Fame. This idea came to my mind from my past attendance at the inaugural British Cycling Hall of Fame ceremony in Manchester in 2010. Following this, in my subsequent visits to the Manchester Velodrome I saw the total whiteness of cyclists on the British Cycling Hall of Fame display at the National Cycling Centre. I felt that I could support British Cycling with better awareness for thinking and looking more broadly to a sense of ethnic diversification when showcasing the best of British people for this very important, publicly facing visual discourse at the publicly funded National Cycling Centre. I'd let both Williams and Burton know about my campaign and discussions with British Cycling, and they backed this.

During my exhibitions in Brighton and at the Herne Hill Velodrome, I collected close to 3000 signatures for my petition, all agreeing that Burton and Williams should be inducted into the British Cycling Hall of Fame. I passed these signatures on to British Cycling management in September 2019, and it was some months later in 2020 that I was invited to join a panel of experts – including the 11-time Paralympic champion Dame Sarah Storey, former BMX World Champion Shanaze Reade, BBC cycling commentator Simon Brotherton, Pro Cycling journalist Sophie Hurcom, UCI off-road manager Simon Burney, SweetSpot director Mick Bennett and British Cycling Board member Kathy Gilchrist – for making recommendations for inductees. We met online on a couple of occasions in our deliberations. Burton was unanimously recommended for induction, but a split decision among the panel meant that Williams was not. In my view, adding one Black face to an exclusive group of by now over 60 British Cycling Hall of Fame cyclists was not enough. I'm hopeful that Williams and more Black cyclists will be added in the future.

My exhibition enabled people to look at the sport of cycling through the lenses of Black champions from across the UK. My book, based on the exhibition, *Desire Discrimination Determination*, extended that knowledge to the life histories of Black champion cyclists from across the USA and Europe, but I knew that there was so much more to learn and know about Black cycling cultures and athletes across the globe.

I hadn't really delved into learning about the USA's Black community cycling culture or African-Caribbean riders' experiences in order to bring forward new knowledge about their lives in relation to the Black-British experiences, and in sharing their imaginations for how cycling could be for them amidst, or in parallel to, the dominance of normalised white systems of being and doing in the sport. I hadn't engaged with African histories and contemporary experiences either, particularly the impact of colonialism and neo-colonialism on Black people in cycling. Given Africa's size and scale, this would need a vast undertaking. But social media has opened new windows for seeing, for conversing, and for giving deeper exploration into the cycling pluriverse. At the click of a button, the connection can be made with Black cycling cultures and communities across the USA, the Caribbean and the African continent. So, in my desire to extend my journey of discovery in cycling through the lenses of Black people's experiences in the sport, the question belonged to me: how far can the bicycle take you?

2

Jesus Christ of the Black cycling community

Learning from past experiences of Black people in their interactions with white cycling cultures can help in seeing how these may relate to learning in the present, for shaping future possibilities and approaches in Black people's self-empowerment and transcendence. Knowing the life and legacy of the USA racing cyclist Marshall 'Major' Taylor (1878–1932) provides an excellent starting point. Conrad and Terry Kerber in their book, *Major Taylor*, discuss how Taylor was named the 'Black Cyclone' by a USA sports media captivated by the power and speed of this Black athlete who'd emerged on to the professional track cycling scene in 1896 as a prodigy, an outstanding talent among his dominant number of white peers. Taylor would often get the better of them, taking the victories in the prestigious races and prize monies that came with that. For this, he was targeted with racial intimidation, physical violence and even murder threats from haters who wanted to put him out of their white circles of the sport. But the hate towards his Blackness and jealousy of his talent would give fuel to his desire and determination to be the best, and this was fulfilled in 1899, in Montreal, Canada, at the World track cycling championships, when Taylor blew his opposition away in the one-mile sprint to become a World Champion in cycling.

Taylor raced his bicycle across the world; in Europe and across Australasia, drawing crowds of thousands of spectators to see him, the Black superstar of the sport. When he retired from professional cycling in 1910 at the age of 32, his life took a drastic turn from the glory heights of his racing days. He suffered poor fortunes including a failed marriage, and failed business ventures, and when he died in 1932 at the age of 53, he was initially buried in an unmarked pauper's grave. This appeared to be a fall from grace, and as though Taylor's deeds as an outstanding racing cyclist would be erased from memories. But his life and legacy were resurrected during the 1970s by his fans and followers and, since then, film documentaries have been created to celebrate the miracles that Taylor performed on the bicycle. Statues, sculptures and murals continue to be commissioned and designed to honour him. Bike trails bearing his name are being opened across the USA. Books, articles, podcasts and exhibitions continue to be created across the world by people inspired by his legendary talent, and his strength and resilience in transcending the white systems and structures of anti-Blackness. Taylor's World Championship-winning year of 1899, his image and his name adorn cycling jerseys of multiple Black cycling clubs across the USA and the world, who view Taylor as their icon; he is revered like a messiah figure, the Jesus Christ of the Black cycling community.

In almost every state and city across the USA, there is a Black-led cycling group created in the name of Major Taylor, from the Major Taylor Cycling Club of Alabama to the Major Taylor Cycling Club San Diego.

Also in California, Major Motion Recreational Cycling, Major Taylor Cycling Club Los Angeles, Major Taylor East Bay; in New York there is Major Taylor Cycling Club of New York/New Jersey and Major Taylor Iron Riders; in New Jersey, Major Taylor Central Jersey and Major Taylor Cycling Club of New Jersey. Taylor is omnipresent in Texas, Tennessee, Ohio, Oklahoma, Florida and Minneapolis. There are more than 40 cycling clubs or organisations in the USA named after Major Taylor and more than 70 cycling clubs or organisations have become formally affiliated with the Major Taylor Association inc., founded in 1998 by residents of Worcester, Massachusetts (Taylor's home town), to preserve and promote Taylor's legacy through educational programmes and events. Across the world, there are established Major Taylor cycling clubs in the UK, Taiwan, France and Kenya. In 2023, plans were announced by the Major Taylor Cycling Club of Chicago, in partnership with the Bronzeville Trail Task Force and the Friends of the Major Taylor Trail, for their icon to be posthumously honoured with the Congressional Gold Medal, the highest civilian award bestowed by the United States of America Congress. Supporting the campaign, Jonathan Jackson, a Black member of the House of Representatives for a district of Illinois, Chicago, said: 'We stand on the shoulders of giants. Marshall Walter "Major" Taylor was such a giant. He faced down the relentless spectre of racial discrimination, both on and off the racetrack. His courage, not just in the realm of sports, but in the greater race of life, set the stage for the victories of the Civil Rights Movement.'

Major Taylor was born in Indianapolis, Indiana, in 1878. As a young boy, he practised tricks on his bicycle. This caught the attention of the white owners of the Hay and Willits bicycle shop, which paid him to hang around the front of the store, dressed in a military uniform, doing trick mounts and stunts to attract business. His attire led locals to nickname him the 'Major'. His work at the popular cycling shop also allowed him to meet and become close friends with some of the best white racing cyclists in the world at the current time, including Louis 'Birdie' Munger and Arthur Zimmerman, who was a two-time world cycling champion in 1893 in different sprint distance events. This early social interaction forged for Taylor an alliance that helped him to cross the Jim Crow colour line in order to compete at some 'whites only' racing events. Still, Taylor's racing ambitions were always going to be restricted by racism, and particularly in the southern states of the USA, where some local promoters would not permit him to compete against white cyclists.

In their book, Conrad and Terry Kerber share what they consider to be one of Taylor's most memorable early cycling victories in 1895, when he was 17, in a 75-mile road race from Indianapolis to Matthews, Indiana. The race was sponsored by the cycling enthusiast George Catterson, a wealthy white businessman. He had become familiar with Taylor's cycling promise through conversations with Birdie Munger and decided to keep Taylor's race entry a secret, for fear of white riders withdrawing and reclaiming their entry fees. On the day of the event, Taylor had kept himself hidden until the start. He then joined the race from behind and sat in at the back. As the race continued, his presence was noticed and he got an angry reception, with riders threatening to kill him if he didn't leave the race immediately. However, rather than climb off his bike and quit, as his opponents desired, he broke away from them instead. The racing conditions had been torrid and humid, but midway, and after Taylor's breakaway, the clouds burst, and the rain poured down heavily. The ground beneath swelled to extreme muddy conditions, so much so that it took its toll on the chasing pack of riders. But Taylor was so far ahead, he was able to ride home solo. It was a superb win, but it showed Taylor that he would face racial slurs and threats to his life from white cyclists. Soon after this race, for his own safety, Taylor switched his immediate attention to competing solely against Black riders over shorter track distances.

At the 1895 Black National Cycling Championships in Chicago, Taylor faced the 'St Louis Flyer', Henry J Stewart, who was known as the undisputed king of Black bike racing. Taylor beat Stewart to become the number one Black champion cyclist of the USA, his first USA title. Still, Taylor was determined to use his talent and powers to challenge the best white cyclists in their exclusive competition spaces. Taylor would appear at white riders-only track meetings. Once the races were over, he would take to the track and ride solo, challenging the long-standing speed records that had been set by the best white riders. And while Taylor's record-breaking efforts gave delight to many of the white spectators, his outstanding performances caused offence to the white riders who witnessed these efforts. Taylor was warned that if he kept showing up to do what he did in front of them and the spectators, he could end up being killed. This Black Cyclone was causing a storm.

News of Taylor's record-breaking feats spread across the USA cycling scene. At 18 years old, Taylor began to work with William Brady, an influential Irish-American theatre actor and producer who was also a sports and entertainment agent for leading talents in the field. In this example of 'interest-convergence', Brady was able to secure for Taylor his professional racing licence from the League of American Wheelmen, the leading national membership organisation for cyclists. Taylor's membership was unprecedented for a Black cyclist. This white sanction – an endorsement given to Black people by white people who hold the power of enablement of access and progression in their social systems – meant that Taylor would now be able to officially race as a registered professional athlete among the best riders in the exclusive white circles of the sport.

Taylor's first professional competitive outing had him shift his focus from short-distance sprint racing and return to endurance with the demanding six-day race at Madison Square Garden in December 1896. This race would be a contest of stamina, with a single rider completing as many laps as possible. Over the six days, Taylor clocked up an incredible 1,732 miles, finishing eighth out of 28 racers. This was a great debut. But he returned his focus to short-distance sprint racing and from here onwards, Taylor went on a winning streak, achieving glorious victory after victory. However, his domination of racing opponents and his growing popularity among fans and the cycling media meant that the verbal and physical threats from his rivals became more deadly than before.

As the writer Seth Davidson puts it: 'The greatest American bike racer of all time, and one of the greatest athletes ever, Major Taylor, was a Black man. Virtually every race he ever started began and ended with racial epithets, threats of violence, and race hatred of the worst kind.' An example of this is during the one-mile Massachusetts Open race at Taunton in September 1897. Taylor would have lost his life had spectators not intervened to prevent him from being strangled to death by an angry rival white rider called William Becker. On this incident, the author and journalist Daniel de Visé writes: 'Rather than disqualify Taylor's attacker, race judges determined that the two men should race again: owing to his injuries, Taylor could not. Officials routinely awarded Taylor second place in races he had clearly won.'

In spite of the continued horrific racial violence directed at Taylor, his desire and determination to be the best could not be thwarted. During 1898–99, he established seven world records – the quarter-mile, the one-third-mile, the half-mile, the two-thirds-mile, the three-quarters-mile, the one-mile, and the two-mile distances. His one-mile world record of 1:41 from a standing start stood for 28 years. He reached a pinnacle of the sport when at the 1899 World Cycling Championship held in Montreal, Canada, in front of 18,000 spectators, he was victorious in the one-mile sprint race ahead of Frenchman Courbe d'Outrelon and American Tom Butler. In 1900, Taylor became the USA Professional Sprint Champion, the title he had coveted for years. One of Taylor's newest rivals was an upcoming and publicly fancied challenger named Eddie Kramer. A match sprint race, organised in June 1900 between Taylor and Kramer, was touted as 'the Great White Hope versus the Black World Champion'. These sorts of racially charged headlines were openly familiar in a time when professional sporting contests were seen as embodying racial meanings in which victory for one side was seen as a racial defeat for the other. On that day, Taylor was able to defeat Kramer.

Despite his world record performances, accolades and being the USA and World Cycling Champion, Jim Crow laws of racial segregation and anti-Blackness in many parts of the USA were crippling his freedom to perform and to thrive commercially, and financially, as a professional Black cyclist. In this situation, it was continuously proving too dangerous for Taylor to race safely.

In 1900, at the age of 22, Taylor left the USA and from 1901 to 1904 he travelled in Europe and Australasia on contracted racing tours. In 1901, Taylor raced across several cities including Vienna, Turin, Rome and Copenhagen. Perhaps the most well-known of Taylor's races during his 1901 European tour were the match sprint contests in Paris between him and Edmond Jacquelin, the darling of French cycling. Jacquelin was not only the French National Sprint Champion, but he was also the 1900 Paris World Championships Sprint Champion. Taylor had not competed in that competition and, likewise, Jacquelin had been absent from the World Championships race in Montreal in 1899 when Taylor was crowned World Champion. So, this was to be the head-to-head clash, best out of three match sprint of the ages – an unofficial World Championship decider between the two titans.

This special event was promoted by Henri Desgrange, founder of the Tour de France, and it took place on 16 May, a public holiday, at the Parc de Princes velodrome in Paris, a popular racing venue of which Desgrange was the director. The day of the race was cold and grey – not conditions Taylor liked – but this didn't prevent 20,000 to 30,000 spectators from filling the velodrome to overflowing. When the races got underway it was Jacquelin who came through strongest, winning the much-anticipated battle of the champions, two-nil. Taylor immediately called for a rematch and Jacquelin accepted. This took place two weeks later, on 27 May, also a public holiday. The crowds filled the Parc des Princes velodrome once more to witness the clash. This time it was Taylor who powered through for a two-nil defeat of Jacquelin. A third meeting would have made a fascinating decider, but unfortunately their conflicting schedules meant this could not happen.

Central to Taylor's strength of character was his religious faith. He was a devout follower of Jesus Christ, and he refused financial incentives to compete on Sundays, reserving it instead as his day of worship. Taylor's belief provided him with the spirit to follow his pathway of providence, and to stand firm against the anti-Blackness he encountered every day in the hostile white world of cycling. As a professional cyclist, he was also a Black businessman and needed to be extra tough to fight for the spoils. As the cycling historian Feargal McKay puts it:

'Taylor endured a lot in his racing career, but he didn't endure it meekly. This was a man who had to fight for everything he won. He didn't just have to be better than the next-best rider in America, he had to be better than all of his rivals combined for that was the way they raced against him, as a combine. Time and again the American authorities tried to stop Taylor from racing, time and again Taylor challenged their authority. This was a man with a core steeled by adversity, a core steeled by the racism he had to endure daily. This was not a man easily cowed.'

From 1895 to 1910, Taylor emerged to become one of history's most remarkable cyclists, but I learned about his life and pursuits late on in my racing career. Nobody I met in my white cycling circles ever mentioned his name, his life or his racing career to me. I'd never seen any books or cycling articles. Maybe the cyclists I knew didn't know about him. Maybe it was because he wasn't a British or European cyclist. But Taylor again came to the forefront of my mind after the men's and women's Tour de France ended in 2022. On my social media feeds, there was a lull in the daily hype and excitement. The more regular Tour de France voices now had nothing new to report on. The party was over for another year and people had gone into holiday mode. However, there was one cycling commentator who, looking to stimulate discussion on social media, created a poll that asked, 'Who is the greatest cyclist?'

After taking suggestions, the commentator narrowed it down to four options: Eddy Merckx, Bernard Hinault, Marianne Vos and 'Other'. The first three are all, in my view, outstanding cycling champions with their own special narratives. However, the possibility of 'Other' being 'the greatest' interested me more. Still, what I perceived would be the leading responses to the poll given by members of the general public came true. Some of their responses were: 'Merckx. It's a no-brainer' and 'The Cannibal [Merckx's racing nickname] of course.' Before the poll ended, I selected 'Other' and wrote, 'Major Taylor – The Black Cyclone'. This didn't attract any attention or endorsement and, as I had expected, Merckx won the poll.

Still, what this cycling poll and some of the public responses to it gave to me was the Eurocentric view on 'greatness' in cycling and cycle racing. The dysconscious racism in this was the tacit acceptance of dominant white cultural norms that have been passed on and learned as unsurpassable ways of knowing cycling; this culturally imbedded narcissism sees nothing else other than itself when describing the sport. The way of seeing and knowing 'greatness' in the sport of cycling has been colonised by an obsessive hegemonic Eurocentric focus on those racing cyclists who achieve their victories on the European stage in the Grand Tours, the Monuments and Classics. I am talking about the inculcation of the populace through the perpetual reproduction of a Eurocentric narrative of cycling hyped by cycling commentators and the cycling media. These are the processes by which a Eurocentric view of cycling maintains its authority and dominant position. Every spring, summer and early autumn, the cycling commentators cheerlead these specific races and popularise the deeds of the cyclists as representing the zenith of human achievement in the sport. For the rider to be victorious in any of these races provides the immortal status of cycling icon. But these Grand Tours, Monuments and Classics are populated year on year by white and European cyclists. On the constructed platform of the world's premier stage for performing in cycling, they are seen and become known as the leading cyclists by achieving 'greatness' according to the generally accepted and unchallenged Eurocentric perspective of the sport at its best.

After the commentator's poll closed, I reached out to some of the leaders of the USA Black cycling community and riders from Major Taylor cycling clubs asking whether they could think of anybody else from yesteryear or today who is equal to, or greater than, Eddy Merckx. Lynne Tolman, Secretary of the Major Taylor Association, replied:

'In my opinion, Major Taylor remains unequalled as a bike racer. No other rider has dominated the competition, and captured the public imagination, the way he did. Major Taylor's legacy in the cycling world is evolving to this day, and not only in the Black cycling community.'

Louis Moore, President of the Major Taylor Bicycling Club of Minnesota, reinforced this perspective when he said:

'There is no-one greater than Major Taylor in cycling. Major Taylor's history is a real inspiration to the modern Black cyclists of today. His history was something that Black folks could identify with and understand what he went through to be a World Champion, because much of his experiences are still part of the modern-day American society.'

I think Tolman and Moore define the legacy of the Black Cyclone well. Taylor's struggle with anti-Black, white-led authorities is the same in modern-day society for many Black people, not just in the USA, but across the world where Black and white people are in interaction, and it is so clear for me to see why a multitude of Black-led cycling clubs across the USA have immortalised him. This is to remind them to use and apply the legacy of his strength, resilience, faith and spirit to transcend the pervasive and racist systems and structures in society that are rooted in anti-Blackness.

In my opinion, greatness comes from actively transcending the human condition in life and perpetually in life after death. I see Major Taylor as the 'Jesus Christ of the Black Cycling Community in the USA'; in his human form, as an outstandingly skilful and powerful Black cyclist that would attract huge public followings to watch him perform miracles on the bike before their eyes; in the afterlife, Taylor is the spiritual force conjured by the Black cycling community as their icon and their idol to follow – the Black Cyclone. Taylor as a force of self-empowerment, resilience and self-belief is the inspiration for millions of people who have come to know his story.

3

Black squares in white circles

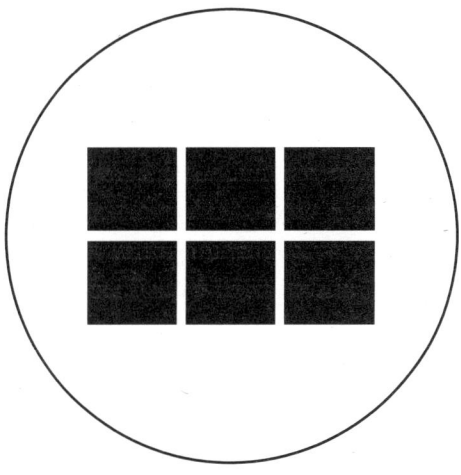

The Black Lives Matter anti-racism protests of 2020 followed the social media-screened police abuse of the Black man George Floyd in Minneapolis, Minnesota, in May 2020. This ugly incident resulted in Floyd's death. In reaction to this horror, millions of people mobilised themselves in cities across the USA to protest publicly. Similar protests happened in UK cities and in many other Western countries. European colonialism of the African continent and Black people's lives has a 600-year legacy and is the root of the modern-day Western ideology of racism. In this, social, economic and political systems have been built to favour and empower the lives, imaginations and ideals of white people. The Black Lives Matter anti-racism protests of 2020 exposed and challenged this racism. The world of cycling did not avoid interrogation.

Some leading sports and cycling brands from the circles of white power in the sport which had never before represented themselves through racial equality or diversity in promoting their products were now keen to do so. This began in full effect on 2 June 2020 – Black Out Tuesday – a solidarity call to action in support of the Black Lives Matter campaign. Leading sports and cycling brands joined in with the Black Out Tuesday action and fitted the Black square symbol of solidarity on to their social media feeds. This reminded me of the mathematical challenge of constructing a square with the area of a given circle, a task proven to be impossible. However, squaring the circle was now possible according to cycling industry dimensions of white sanction.

Black Out Tuesday occurred during the COVID-19 worldwide pandemic. During lockdown, I had been following some interesting new stories and developments on social media in which Black cyclists across the USA were forming collectives and championing cycling as their main social activity. Some of these groups were also using the words of Black power, Black unity and Pan-Africanism in their names, for example Black Watts Cycling from New Jersey, Kings Rule Together (KRT) and Queens Rule Together (QRT) in Philadelphia, and Red Bike and Green from Atlanta, Georgia.

What I was seeing in the USA was similar in many ways to what I had witnessed in the UK in London, just before and during the COVID-19 lockdown and around the time of the Black Lives Matter protests. There had been a growth in Black-led cycling collectives here too, with names such as Black Riders Association, Black Unity Ride and the Black Cyclists Network. I wrote about this phenomenon in my book, *Desire, Discrimination, Determination*. I saw them as 'New tribes in cycling', where each new cycling group seemed to be being voiced and driven by a distinctive leader as their spokesperson.

So, with the Black Lives Matter anti-racism discourses trending across the media and an explosion of interest from some leading white-owned sports and cycling brands, all keen to publicise their moral sentiment and new positioning in advancing 'diversity', many of the new Black-led groups from London secured cycling brand partnership deals, and their cycling jerseys became stamped with the logos of white-owned cycling technology companies and white-owned cycling sports food companies.

In this example of 'interest-convergence', were these new Black and white relationships the genuine beginnings of cycling solidarity for delivering racial inclusion and anti-racism in cycling? Or were they simply opportunistic, a superficial and tokenistic response to Black Lives Matter? Race-diversity discourses appearing in cycling through white-owned cycling brands and new Black cycling group partnerships have been welcomed as positive, but simultaneously viewed as being for show only. Take the former professional cyclist from the USA, Rahsaan Bahati, who told *Velonews*, 'I mean, there's brands that use Black people in their ads and try to use diversity in their campaigns. For me, that's always been a checked box. Like, "There are more Black people buying bikes than ever, we better put them in the ads."'

I spoke directly with another respected Black cyclist, the former professional from the USA, Eric Saunders, explaining to him that I saw these new Black cycling groups becoming aligned with some leading white-owned cycling companies and promoting their products as a 'Black squares fitting in white circles' solution. When considering his own small cycling business in relation to the power held by larger influential, white-owned cycling brands, Saunders gave me a useful view on their monopolising of new Black cyclists as their ambassadors:

'I think the purpose was to get attention . . . and white-owned brands got it. I am all about Black people getting paid. I would never want to take away an opportunity to earn from anyone. White people own all the brands . . . so what other way is there? Black-owned cycling businesses are likely to be small and not be structured in a way that the system would recognise. I ran into this with my company – Memory Pilot. So, there is a lot that needs to happen before I can compete with large companies for ambassadors . . . it's always a question of who has and can continue to secure access to resources . . . attention is a resource . . . by taking it all, those with greatest power and resource in cycling are guaranteeing that there isn't going to be a Black owner competing for that attention.'

'Attention is a resource' was key thinking that I took from Saunders, and I became more interested in these new relationships of influence in the Black squares in white circles equation. I used social media to contact cycling leaders and groups from the Black communities of New York, New Jersey, Philadelphia and Charlotte, North Carolina, and Miami, Florida. I arranged to meet some of them to talk about this in the USA, face to face. The COVID-19 worldwide lockdown was coming to an end. I also wanted to take the opportunity to share the stories of Black cycling champions in the sport that I had researched and written about, so, in February 2022, just after New York City had lifted its COVID-19 Omicron restrictions for social gatherings, I was on the plane heading over from the UK.

I had never visited the USA and I never had any big desire or reason to before this new interest of mine. I had seen enough of it on the television since the 1970s to make my sense of it, particularly in relation to my social identity as a Black man. I'm not generalising about all Black or all white Americans when I reflect, think and speak about the USA, but, when I was younger, only seeing and knowing about the USA through what I saw on TV showed me that there were significant possibilities for Black people as pioneers or leaders in sports like athletics, boxing and American football, or through innovative musical forms such as rock 'n' roll, blues, jazz, soul and hip-hop. Still, my viewing and learning about the place was generally presented by white people who had the power and control. I knew that there were major problems with being a Black person in the USA, even when you were famous and had become a millionaire through sport, music or entertainment. For example, the consequences of World Heavyweight Champion boxer Muhammad Ali convicted and stripped of his titles for refusing to be drafted into the USA military in 1967 for the war in Vietnam is just one example of the silencing of a powerful Black man in his prime by the white-led national authorities. I knew that many more Black men who were outspoken about how the USA's racist social and economic system disadvantages Black people have been killed by the white-led national authorities. This long history of white violence against Black people in the USA has been ugly. I'd also been educated about Black people in the USA defying the white narrative of their subordination through the radical words and music of the blues, jazz, soul and hip-hop that I had listened to, and by reading accounts of resisting the disease of racism in the USA through the writings of Frederick Douglass, William Du Bois, Richard Wright, Martin Luther King and Malcolm X.

When I arrived in Manhattan, New York, it did not occur to me that I'd chosen to stay in accommodation that was situated opposite the famous Madison Square Garden on 8th Avenue, but I stood outside in awe, and thought about its famous purpose-built velodrome of the past and Major Taylor, the Black Cyclone, racing there on his professional debut in 1896. After I'd checked in, I went to find myself a taxi to take me to the Rapha Cycling Clubhouse, the venue I'd chosen for my meeting and talk. I stumbled along the street with my two suitcases full of exhibition materials. I crossed over to the other side of 33rd Street West, catching my first glimpse of the iconic Empire State Building. Immediately, *King Kong* flashed into my mind. That fictional film portrayal of a huge gorilla as a Black monstrosity, extracted from the heart of Africa's darkness, loose on the New York streets, causing a frenzy and screams of white fear. I chuckled to myself at the madness of it all. Instantly, I was brought back to the moment. Cars and lorries were flashing past. I began to cross the street, not realising that I should be looking right instead of left. I quickly switched my head the other way to see more cars and huge trucks heading towards me with their headlights blinding me. I raised my hand as if to shout 'Stop!' as I rushed over to the other side. I clocked a yellow taxi and waved at the driver. He nodded. I threw my cases on to the back seats of the taxi and jumped in.

We hit the back of traffic on 5th Avenue and slowed to walking pace. I noticed that we were near the entrance to the Empire State Building. I saw large wording on the windows promoting a ground floor to observatory experience at $95 US dollars for 15 minutes. Next, as the taxi moved forwards, in my face, with bulbous eyes looking at me through the window, was the beast, King Kong, albeit as a huge cardboard cut-out. I laughed out loud in shock and thought to myself, 'King Kong as the Empire State Building brand ambassador, as the commercial influencer.' Suddenly, the taxi driver punched the horn of his vehicle and cursed the cars ahead. We were able to move on.

The flyer for my Desire, Discrimination, Determination US tour

When we finally arrived at the venue, I walked away from an extremely expensive fare thinking we had only been driving around in circles. I stepped into the Rapha Cycling Clubhouse and immediately started to buzz with excitement at the thought of what was to come. I left my exhibition cases at the side of the venue entrance.

'Can I help you?' I heard as a call from the barista.

'Thanks! No, I am just here for looking around!' I responded. I didn't really want to introduce myself to anybody so immediately. Then almost a few seconds later as I moved into the store, from a different direction, and behind cycling apparel, 'Hi. Hey! Do you need any help?'

'Ah. Yes. In a moment. I am just here checking things out.'

I moved on. But the continued reception of willingness for me to be assisted didn't cease.

'Are you OK?' came another offer of support.

There were more staff than actual customers in the store. In fact, I was the only visitor at the time. I didn't want to believe this to be some form of oxymoronic polite hostile surveillance of me. So, I gave in.

'Hello. Actually. Yes. I am Dr Marlon. . .'

'Moncrieffe! Dr Marlon?' came from the spitting image of a young Lance Armstrong, in my face – high cheekbones, piercing blue eyes, skinny. I was thrown by this, and I froze at the possibility. But of course, no. No! Not working at the Rapha Cycling Clubhouse in New York City.

'Yes. OK. I am just checking things out because I am here to share my book tomorrow.'

'Yes! Hi. These came for you today.'

The flyers that I had made last-minute and sent over from the UK to meet me here in New York City had arrived.

'Yes! They made it.'

'Great! Are you the manager here?'

'One of them. Hey! Dr Marlon! We're real excited about this talk! Thank you. We have always felt that we have been ahead of the game, you know, when it comes to talking cycling, society, and fusing things together and. . .'

As he went on, I found myself drawn to the wonderful interior design of the venue. Cycling jerseys neatly lined on the rails. Traditional coloured cotton jerseys framed beautifully and hanging from the bricked interior walls. The large photographic visuals promoting Black-faced, Brown-faced and white-faced cycling models all posing together in style, in their Rapha kits – a 21st-century version of a 20th-century United Colors of Benetton collective.

'. . . and so, thank you for coming over!'

Lance came to a pause, seeking my response, blue eyes piercing me. 'Ah yes. Yes. It's great! It's great! It really is. It is so nice to be here, in the USA, in New York City. Thank you! Let's talk some more, but can you direct me to the toilet, please?'

'Sure. Sure. Yes, just down there on the left,' he pointed.

As I walked across the store, I noted the framed posters presenting images of European cycling classics and their cycling heroes. I couldn't see much of the local Black cycling groups, though. The Brooklyn Red Caps came to mind. I'd read about this seminal New York Black-led cycling group of the 1980s. They'd meet at the entrance of Prospect Park every weekend for their long rides out of the city, into the hills and back. They included top riders such as James Joseph of Guyana, who competed at the 1980 and 1984 Summer Olympics. I was also looking for an image of Nelson Vails, the 1984 Olympic Track Sprint silver medallist, a recognisable name and legend of USA cycling, who was originally from New York. I walked on, clocking the vivid design of the L39ION of Los Angeles team cycling jersey owned by two Black professional criterium racing cyclists, the brothers Justin and Cory Williams. The jersey was hanging on the clothing rail for sale at a mere $175! Well, in terms of Black people squaring circles with white businesses, at least this item gave the Black cycling imagination a presence in the store. But as I walked on, I thought to myself, 'That's bloody expensive! I wonder how many Black kids from the Bronx could afford it?' But then maybe this sort of item was for the Black middle-class cycling enthusiasts of New York or anyone else who had that sort of money to spend on a cycling jersey and was inspired by L39ION of Los Angeles and their Black leaders.

Nelson Vails

I found the toilet. It was a small space, tucked away, out of the immediate sight of customers. I walked in, closed the door behind me. 'Aha!', I exclaimed to myself. There it was: a small image of the Black cycling icon, Nelson Vails, along with brief details of his cycling story, on the wall of the men's toilet.

———

The next evening, I described my discovery to the audience at my talk, highlighting how the presence and representation of Black people have been generally marginalised in the sport of cycling. I could see that they were with me in feeling that the story of the Black cycling icon of New York, Nelson Vails, could be better placed.

The venue was packed to the brim and the panel included figures such as Dereka Hendon, club president of Major Taylor Iron Riders; Mel Corbett, founding member and club historian, also of Major Taylor Iron Riders; Chris Harvell, Aquil Jannah and Chad Bennett, founding members of New Jersey's Black Watts Cycling Club; Malaku 'Prince' Mekonnen, founder of Team Cycling Royalty; Ajoa Abrokwa of She is Fit and Focused from Philadelphia; and Babalola Ajisafe of Century Road Club Association and the Major Taylor Development Cycling Team. Although the venue was dominated by Black people involved in cycling, this was a multi-ethnic New York audience, and white and Asian people involved in cycling themselves or connected to a local ethnically inclusive cycling organisation like Star Track Cycling joined us, too.

I spoke with joy and passion about my interest in the growth of the Black cycling community across the USA, in relation to what I knew about the rise of an empowered Black cycling community in London, following the Black Lives Matter protests. I told them that I was interested to know their thoughts about some of the more renowned white-owned cycling brands who had given communications of support to Black Out Tuesday, when previously there seemed to have been little or nothing from cycling in the way of championing diversity or anti-racist messaging. So, how did these new communications go down with people? Ajoa Abrokwa gave a balanced response to the Black squares in white circles equation when she said:

'I believe that there are some pros to having people of colour, Black people specifically "serving" as ambassadors for these white brands. To me, it provides visibility for groups of people that have long lived in the shadows. Having Black people in these spaces also lends itself to a level of representation, diversity and inclusion that is often very much needed. This representation allows for the creation of opportunity for those that would like to be on display within the sport.

'However, in my short experience in cycling, I have seen issues that have arisen from the approach that is taken when identifying who and how the ambassadors are chosen and displayed. Unfortunately, in some instances these brands both tokenize and exploit Black cyclists. They promise very little for self-serving gains. I have also seen corporations and brands target people and groups, communities that they believe need them to "get in the door". It's sometimes very sad to watch, because the brands talk about big change and support, but deliver the minimum. However, they take their pictures and have the assets they need to illustrate a façade.'

Superficiality in the Black squares in white circles equation leading to the exploitation of Black people was also a concern for Malaku Mekonnen, who said:

'Many of the big white-owned companies that seek brand ambassadors don't have the best interests of people of colour but have rather found a better way to sell their products. When the big cyclist boom happened and masses of people of colour got on bikes and made cycling look very attractive, the big bike companies found a new way to make money and make up for their losses. Cue in all the Black men and women – make them ambassadors of our bikes.'

An insight into the manipulation of Black people by the leading white-owned cycling brands, which project a discourse of diversity and a message of racial inclusion, while backstage, out of sight, perpetuating racial inequalities, was shared by Babalola Ajisafe, when he said:

'Working as an ambassador with any of the mainstream brands that tend to all be predominantly white-owned gives you a minor foot in the door . . . Even more important than the access to the product is the access to information and upcoming new tech trends . . . Long term would be if that foothold would progress to an actual seat at the table in order to help make decisions on how the organisations can properly help grow the brands in under-sourced communities that could use the product, and their investment in the product would also be financially beneficial to the company at large. Sadly, we tend to not see the status of such a mutually beneficial partnership come to fruition.

'The con to this kind of arrangement is that the brands now have a Black or Brown face on hand to go to and claim diversity when and if they are questioned for their poor business practices to people of colour, inactivity in urban spaces, inability to follow up on promises made to people and communities of colour. A person of colour can quickly become a poster child for diversity on the surface of any cycling brand yet hide the nasty underbelly of what truly goes on behind closed doors and in their board meetings.'

These were all stark responses, all chiming with what Bahati and Saunders had sensed in the Black squares in white circles equation claim. Yes, this was a positive response to Black Lives Matter by white-owned cycling brands, but at the same time requiring checking for its depth, in recognising the power relationship between white-owned cycling brands and Black people, many of whom are new to cycling. Black people in cycling, especially those coming new to the sport during lockdown, may have been drawn in by being seen to be associated with influential white-owned brands. The marketing benefit for the white-owned brands is Black community grassroots visibility for their products. As Eric Saunders had told me, 'Attention is a resource.' Black people as brand ambassadors for white cycling products can influence the behaviour of other Black people. Some people have called this out as 'exploitation', but where the leading white-owned brands in cycling provide bikes, bike technologies, bike clothing, branded helmets and sports foods freely to those Black cyclists, and pay them handsomely as brand ambassadors, perhaps exploitation is not even considered as an issue; it's a partnership and business is business.

The irony of our meeting to discuss the Black squares in white circles equation is that, as a dominant group of Black people, we held our conversation in a white-owned space. This meeting was totally at my instigation, and I made the decision about the venue. Everyone whom I invited were, in my view, very pleased to be involved. In the evening, we were very warmly welcomed by our hosts, who were learning to facilitate a sense of 'inclusion' in cycling. For some in cycling, the increased use of Black cyclists to advertise white-owned cycling companies may be about fostering ethnic diversity in a sport renowned for its whiteness, but as I have found from the responses given to my questions, there are complexities around inclusion and partnership, and how these new relationships function. If inclusion and partnership means Black people fitting in with the already existing moulds of white imagination of the sport, then race equality is not advanced.

I thought our coming together was unique and valuable. Still, on reflection, with all New York's powerful history of Black-led rallies and leadership for social justice and transformation in society, perhaps the neater fit for our conversational space would have been a Black-owned community cycling clubhouse near Marcus Garvey Park in Harlem, where perhaps we would have generated a more radical conversation around the complex Black squares in white circles equation.

4

When Tao took the knee

Before the start of the Tour de France in 2020 I wrote in *The Conversation* that it would be a huge surprise if we saw any riders taking the knee during this event or raising their fists to show solidarity with the huge wave of Black Lives Matter anti-racism protests across the world. Despite the restrictions on sport during the pandemic, support for the anti-racism message was being communicated in popular professional sports such as football, cricket, rugby, basketball and baseball. Still, I was doubtful that professional cycling would join in with this – and I was correct. In the aftermath of lockdown, UCI World Tour racing action (there's a hierarchy of races and the World Tour sits at the top) began again with the Strade Bianche. This is one of the spring Classics and it's normally held in early March, but the exceptional circumstances meant that in 2020 it was held on 1 August. However, professional cycling still failed to offer the messages of solidarity with anti-racism that other world-leading sports had given.

Later on that month, on 29 August, when the Tour de France began in Nice, the silence from professional cycling continued. It was after three weeks of racing, on 20 September, the final day of the event, and after some criticism in the cycling media about the way the Tour de France was ignoring Black Lives Matter, that at the beginning of the processional stage from Mantes-la-Jolie to Paris, several of the riders emerged together with anti-racist messages scribbled on their COVID-19 facemasks.

This anti-racist communication was very different to the display of raised fists and knee-taking being performed across other sports, and not all riders from the Tour de France peloton took part. I remember the reaction given to this anti-racist gesture from some cycling commentators and social media observers describing what they saw as underwhelming, pathetic and completely hopeless and embarrassing. Still, in my view, what the riders did on that final day was at least something for the world to see, and better than showing nothing. Among the riders that took part in the anti-racist demonstration was the B&B Hotels–Vital Concept rider Kévin Reza, the only Black cyclist in the peloton. He'd been calling out for action against racism in professional cycling based on his own experiences of abuse. In discussion with Sky Sports, when asked about the action taken by the riders on the final day of the 2020 Tour de France, Reza appeared to be pleased with this when he said, 'It's not like I couldn't do that for years, but I was given the opportunity to do it on the biggest race in the world. This is something that makes me happy and that also allows us to spark debate.' But no debate followed, and Reza's initial optimism gave in to realism when some months later he said that he didn't have an answer for what the peloton could do. He acknowledged that it was 'complicated' as in a peloton of 200 riders, everyone could have 'their own debates, their own thoughts' making it 'difficult to tell everyone to stick together on sensitive issues like this'. Reza's presence on the 2020 Tour de France peloton provided some influence in triggering their public communication of anti-racism, but it seemed that this message needed a more robust, influential and highly respected leader of the 200 riders from the Tour de France. Speaking in the *Guardian,* the INEOS Grenadiers manager Dave Brailsford pointed to the action and example that the Black-British F1 World Champion Lewis Hamilton shaped for his sport, saying, 'If cycling had somebody of Lewis's profile and passion, maybe we'd have a greater impact.' In the same article, the American rider Peter Stetina said, 'Cycling doesn't currently have a Black superstar . . . I think it's important to allow Black voices to take the lead and for the rest of us to support them.'

A few months later, a superstar cyclist did emerge to take a lead on the issue, but this was not a Black cyclist. Step forward the white British cyclist Tao Geoghegan Hart of INEOS Grenadiers, and the winner of the 2020 Giro d'Italia. In December 2020, he shared with the BBC his intentions to 'improve' racial 'diversity' in sport when he said:

'There's a lot to be done in diversity . . . I believe London can be the key to that . . . It was such a privilege to go to school there and grow up there because of all of the incredible variety of people I came across . . . '

When I read this, I saw that to some extent, Geoghegan Hart's brief description of his early life background chimed with my own, given that I am from London too. I also lived and went to school among a broad ethnic mix of people who were from across the four UK nations, from the African continent, the Caribbean, Asia and Europe. That's what the multicultural space of London gives. To me, Geoghegan Hart's reflections on his multi-ethnic socialisation and his publicly disclosed interest and intent to become 'part of' change implied his calling out of how cycling's privileged access, participation, representation and success in the sport aligned with being a white person.

Next, in February 2021, Geoghegan Hart drew further media and public attention through an Instagram post of himself in his INEOS Grenadiers kit, taking the knee. There was no raised fist to accompany the gesture and, curiously, Geoghegan Hart's action was away from public sight. Unlike the public performances we had seen given at professional football, cricket and rugby matches as spectators returned to stadiums after the COVID-19 lockdown, Geoghegan Hart took the knee alone, in an empty football playing field on Hackney Marshes in London. In the Instagram post he spoke with humility in describing his work as, 'A job that I see as a huge privilege and my dream', stating his personal intent to take action on calling out inequality in the sport: 'Cycling has a problem with diversity and inclusivity.'

My immediate thoughts and feelings towards the fervent media and public applause towards Geoghegan Hart's communication was confusion. Geoghegan Hart was representing himself, and by the fact he was wearing an INEOS Grenadiers kit, he was representing his team too. But I remained perplexed, as I wrote on social media – 'But, there is nobody there!' This gesture was in my view an impotent communication by the choice of environment in which it was made: on a football pitch on the Hackney Marshes, and in solitude. This came across to me as a publicity stunt in its definition of seeking to attract attention, for a good reason. But, it just seemed to me to be without depth. I wrote about the confusion in what I saw in an *Advancing Anti-Racism in Cycling* article that I published in February 2021, posing the question in the title: 'How do we applaud anti-racist action in cycling beyond a sense of tokenistic superficiality?' Geoghegan Hart said, 'I have not done enough' and spoke of his intentions to lead the cause of diversity. He concluded, 'I'll always look to you out there for inspiration, advice and ideas on how I can try to contribute to moving this incredible sport forward.' It was good to hear this, but for me it was unclear as to who 'you out there' meant. In my view, sharing some sense of knowledge towards the Black-British-led activism and work in the sport for championing ethnic diversity, inclusion and anti-racism 'out there' that had been occurring in London and across the country way before the staged Hackney Marshes photo shoot would have been a better start to the campaign.

In reflecting on what Brailsford and Stetina had both suggested and said earlier about the need for a leading Black voice in cycling that the sport could support and follow, step forward the Black professional cyclist Justin Williams of USA (now Belize), a well-known figure in the Black cycling community across the USA. In October 2021 he posted on social media a photograph of him from *Rouleur* magazine that showed him wearing his stars and stripes USA champion's jersey, head tucked down, and fist clenched high in a Black Power salute. In doing this, Williams was also alone and away from public sight, in what seemed to be a photo studio. His message on social media was:

'I look at this photo of me, a Black man in a gold chain and American flag in 2021, still having to feel this way and having to very much relate to what people in the past have fought and died for – and we're still here fighting and dying for it. The fight is not over.'

I saw Williams' message and method of communication as being a publicity stunt too, just like Geoghegan Hart's, in its definition of seeking to attract attention. However, the difference in language between Geoghegan Hart and Williams is that the latter uses emotion to personalise his experience of anti-Black racism in connection to his people in the past, seeing this as his personal struggle in the present. Still, I perceived that any power of intent behind Williams' communication could pass by some people's minds, simply in what has become a relative norm of seeing a Black sportsman from the USA raising his fist in defiance. Critics might acknowledge this as a powerful gesture, but also as nothing new or sensational in comparison to the white guy.

Williams and Geoghegan Hart were both using their platforms to make a statement about the same issues of racism in sport and in cycling. However, a key difference in public amplification that I saw given to each of their messages was when the white-British cyclist's performance and accompanying narrative was described by the *Guardian* in March 2021 as an 'exclusive' story. Geoghegan Hart spoke of taking inspiration from his hero, the Black-British Formula 1 World Champion racing driver Lewis Hamilton, who, throughout the 2020 race season, had been protesting systemic racism by taking the knee and raising his fist before the races and on the podium in front of millions of people worldwide. Hamilton's were peaceful and generally staged protests, publicity stunts in seeking to attract attention to the cause, and some of his white peers sometimes joined him in this. But Geoghegan Hart also had the world at his feet because of the attention that he created at the 2020 Giro d'Italia, and his maiden Grand Tour victory significantly increased his public profile. Raising a fist and going down on the knee at the Giro d'Italia finale in Milan, Italy, while wearing the pink winner's jersey, could have created a sporting and political moment of the ages; one which I believe could have been just as iconic as the actions taken by the Black track and field athletes Tommy Smith and John Carlos of the USA during their medal ceremony at the 1968 Olympic Games in Mexico City. Both used the raised fist as a human rights salute in relation to systematic and institutional racism inflicted on Black people across the world. The 2020 Giro d'Italia victory podium was for Geoghegan Hart, and he didn't have to do anything for anyone apart from himself, but imagine if he had taken the knee and raised his fist in front of a world audience, just like his hero Lewis Hamilton had been doing on a regular basis. I think this would have attracted huge waves of haters, slating him for wokeness, seeking to destroy his cycling career. On the other hand, by taking the knee and raising his fist in Milan in front of millions of people worldwide, Geoghegan Hart would have been remembered forever as the 2020 Giro d'Italia victor who used the world stage to call out systemic and structural racism in cycling. Geoghegan Hart may have become a white cycling legend in the minds of some people, like a Bob Geldof Band-Aid-feed-the-world-save-the-starving-Africans-of-Ethiopia sort of figure.

When Geoghegan Hart spoke to the *Guardian* about taking the knee, he said:

'I decided to do it before my first race, but away from the race itself. I felt it could be less impactful in the melee and chaos of a bike race start-line . . .'

There were mixed views on Geoghegan Hart's knee-taking gesture among the Black people in cycling that I spoke with, particularly on what it was supposed to signify, and its intended impact. I asked some Black leaders in cycling how did it made them feel when Tao took the knee and to what extent they thought this action could genuinely bring transformations to the sport. When I was in New York City, Babalola Ajisafe told me that he was positive about Geoghegan Hart's knee-taking gesture:

'Honestly, I was surprised, it made me feel that at least we have some allies in the pro peloton who see the issues being faced at large in the public media landscape as well as the micro-environment of cycling sport. I had my reservations as to what his motives were, but such is irrelevant. I would hope to see and hear of anyone taking such a stance in the past, present and future have a plan on how they can help bring light to and combat systemic racism in all walks of life, but for our athletes, let's start with the immediate domain in which they reside and just try to tackle the cycling sport landscape and go from there.'

Malaku Mekonnen of Philadelphia gave his view on white-led interventions to fix the issues of racial inequality when he told me:

'I feel that many of the racist ideas and attitudes that have plagued the world have come from the Eurocentric scope and have been perpetuated by people of that persuasion. So, it will take people of European ancestry to come and rectify the problems that they put forth. I think few other professional cyclists didn't follow [Tao in taking the knee] because ignorance is bliss. Even if they claim that they aren't racist themselves, they are culturally ignorant and have no acknowledgement that there is a problem, it's not their concern. White supremacy is a benefit to white people and has all its wealth and benefits in the bag for those who keep it up and hold it.'

Some Black people will be critical of white public figures that emerge from nowhere to suddenly take to the moral high ground in order to be seen and known leading the world to change on racism. The distrust in the white-led intervention increases when the continuous media narrative on this systemic racism becomes suffocated by the hype in the applause given to the heroic intervention of the white protagonist. Geoghegan Hart gave further indication to his next steps when he said in his publicly shared Instagram post:

'I will be taking action with @hbaxeon by sponsoring an under-23 rider to race with the team this summer. I hope this can be the beginning of a joint effort to increase racial diversity within the amazing sport of Cycling. I will work with @axelmerckx and his team in the coming months to identify, coach and mentor the person, and athlete, to join the team on August 1st.'

With this announcement came an eruption of social media lauding:

'NOW you're officially a legend. Well done mate!' – Fan 1.
'Thank you for doing this and actually doing something with a long-term plan.' – Fan 2.
'Huge respect young man. Role model.' – Fan 3.
'Leading from the front.' – Fan 4.
'Lead the way dude.' – Fan 5.
'This is amazing, and I hope others follow.' – Fan 6.
'You're from da endz as da mandem say. Nothin but admiration for your generosity let's make it happen for someone who may not ordinarily get the chances.' – Fan 7.

Cycling media cheerleaders also began to sing, dance and praise in their excitement:

'Tao Geoghegan Hart has taken action to improve diversity in cycling.' *Cycling Weekly.*
'Tao Geoghegan Hart has reiterated his stance for more diversity and inclusivity in professional cycling.' *Cyclingnews.*

WHEN TAO TOOK THE KNEE

'Tao Geoghegan Hart to sponsor individual rider in battle for diversity in cycling.' *Cyclist.*

Even Kévin Reza was applauding and describing Geoghegan Hart as a 'gentleman', adding, 'It's strong, it's a very good start and then it also encourages young people who cannot afford financially to be able to reach the highest level.'

Many of these responses did not contemplate critically this intervention which to me epitomised the exclusive power of white sanction – the power of determining and enabling Black people to access white systems and structures. What I was seeing was like Roald Dahl's privileged and wealthy 'Willy Wonka' character offering a 'golden ticket' to a poor 'Black' Charlie to enter the World Tour cycling factory for a brief moment only.

The claim made by axeoncycling.com is that in the selection process to become Geoghegan Hart's mentee, 'over a dozen applications were considered'. Given the heightened cycling headlines and public declarations from Geoghegan Hart about his intervention, it would also have been interesting, I think, for the public to know more about the applicants to this special opportunity. But this information was not shared with the public. I would have liked to have known more about those riders too: Were they British riders? Did any riders from the African continent apply? In my view and knowledge of the British scene, there was not much out there, if anything at all in elite cycling in terms of aspirant and active Black riders. There was only really one recognisable Black-British rider who I thought had a chance of being the chosen one and that was Red Walters. He had spent the 2019 season racing for the UCI Continental team, Vitus Pro Cycling Team p/b Brother. At the time of the Geoghegan Hart and Hagens Berman Axeon announcement, he was representing the newly formed Black-British-led group, Black Cyclists Network, and was their only rider to have ever raced competitively at elite level road racing. Walters was also individually sponsored by the sports nutrition food product company, Science in Sport, which was also incidentally in partnership with Geoghegan Hart's INEOS Grenadiers team at the time. In my view, the unofficial betting odds were extremely short on Walters receiving the pick from Geoghegan Hart and Hagens Berman Axeon. Of course, this happened. Of the process to being selected Walters told me:

'The Axeon deal came about through Tao's sponsored stagiaire programme. I sent a massive CV. I had it in the back of my mind. In May and June, they put another statement out saying they were still looking for riders and I thought, "Damn, that means me out of it," but two weeks later, Tao asked for my WhatsApp number, and it went from there. When Tao told me I'd been selected, I was honestly over the moon. I can't emphasise enough how hard I tried to get this kind of opportunity.'

To be fair, from what I saw from following him on Instagram, Walters had been very dedicated and determined to grow in the sport. I'd been watching his progress since he came on the cycling scene as a fourth category novice rider with the Hampshire-based cycling club, Sotonia CC. I asked Walters, when Tao took the knee, did this really have any genuine impact in transforming attitudes to racism, diversity and inclusion in the sport, other than immediately providing the opportunity to test ride with the Hagens Berman Axeon Cycling Team? He said:

'I think taking the knee is a sign of acknowledgement that racism exists in the world we live in today as well as in the years gone by. In other sports with more Black representation, it's easier for white athletes to join the movement when it's already been established in a given sport, like football for example. If a few Black athletes on a team decide to take a knee, it's easy for the rest of the team to join in solidarity. Not to say it's insincere, but the choice is an easy one. By contrast, in cycling, where we have very few Black athletes in the top echelon of the sport, it takes more initiative to decide to do something.

'In Formula 1, for example, I don't believe the anti-racism campaign would have existed without Lewis Hamilton, if not directly from his own actions, just by virtue of the success he's achieved in the sport. I applaud Tao for being one of the first white pro cyclists to talk about these issues, and for taking action, and hopefully over time it will inspire others to do similar. I think if a Black rider and their team decides to take action, then we might see a lot of white pros repeat. Another factor could also be the fear of not doing the right thing. There are definitely people out there who might agree with Tao, but don't know how they could do something similar without someone to lead the way. There will also be people out there who simply don't feel it's their place or problem.'

This is a broad and sincere response from Walters that in some ways echoes the thoughts given by Kévin Reza in that there will 'not always be the same opinions' among riders in the peloton about whether there is an issue or not to do with race and racism in cycling, and there are people 'who simply don't feel it's their place or problem.' But then again, Walters credits Geoghegan Hart as being 'one of the first white pro cyclists' to take the knee and potentially a trailblazer, opening the way for a fuller addressing of racism. Walters' view is that this gesture from Geoghegan Hart may lead to similar interventions and action from his white peers.

Walters discussed the two races that he rode at World Tour level for Hagens Berman Axeon as, ' . . . a crazy, crazy experience. I didn't feel out of my depth from the start, but I look to my left and there is Julian Alaphilippe and Fernando Gaviria, my idols, and they are just there.' He added: 'I would say I gained more experience in those two races than the previous two years, maybe even three. It was such a different environment at those races, the skill of the riders was just so much higher.' However, the Hagens Berman Axeon Cycling Team experience evaporated quickly, and Walters was not retained for racing at World Tour level. That was the end of it.

For the 2022 season, Walters signed with the British-based team Ribble Weldtite Pro Cycling. He also used UK and Grenadian dual citizenship to his advantage to race at international level as the Grenadian National Champion and represent this nation at the Commonwealth Games in Birmingham in 2022.

In taking the knee and raising his voice, I think Geoghegan Hart was generous and brave to use his public profile and power as a Grand Tour winner to call for transformation in the white-dominated sport, and Geoghegan Hart received deserved applause from both Black and white cyclists and cycling fans for this. I think he sought something better for cycling, but I think all of this energy and effort could have gone further than it actually did. What a shame that this project could not be sustained in the long term.

5

'Go back to your own country!'

'Go back to your own country!' are words that I know very well, particularly from watching television back in the 1990s, when England were playing football at Wembley. John Barnes of Liverpool FC was the sole Black player on that England team. Every time the ball came to him, there were boos and monkey noises from some of the spectators in the stands. And these noises came from England supporters. It was outrageous. Barnes was substituted. He seemed to be playing well enough, but at least being withdrawn from sight saved him from any further abuse. Here was a Black man trying his best to represent

England. 'Go back to your own country!' was the message of hate he faced that evening.

Three individual kicks of a football in the right place in the men's European football championships 2020 final (played in 2021) between England and Italy could have seen Marcus Rashford, Bukayo Saka and Jadon Sancho – three Black-British men – exalted as national sporting heroes for the rest of their lives, but they all missed their penalties. There was an incredible racist backlash at their failures. The Black man of England made a mess of what the white man of England had been dreaming of for England since 1966. Football didn't come home, but racism did. The *Independent* reported, 'Within minutes of his [Saka's] shot being saved, he received abuse on his Instagram account, which was flooded with monkey emojis', by racists posting abusive recordings. The *Guardian* and *Sky News* reported how racists livestreamed themselves on Facebook posting offensive rants about Rashford, Sancho and Saka to publicly vilify them.

For all the knee-taking gestures in football, performed to show solidarity with Black Lives Matter in 2020, and for all of the Kick It Out and Show Racism the Red Card discourses of anti-racism, the undercurrents of racial hatred towards the Black man representing the majority white nation exploded like geysers into the atmosphere as a reminder of what is hidden under the surface of things.

There has been an increased selection of Black footballers performing for England's national team after John Barnes during the 1990s, in fact over 100 great footballers including the likes of David Rocastle (Arsenal); Ian Wright (Crystal Palace, Arsenal, West Ham United, Burnley); Paul Ince (Manchester United, Internazionale Milano, Liverpool, Middlesbrough); Rio Ferdinand (West Ham United, Leeds United, Manchester United); Jude Bellingham (Birmingham City, Borussia Dortmund, Real Madrid). Ince and Ferdinand have captained England's national team. These Black footballers are champions of England and champions across Europe for their club teams, but when thinking about cycling and representation for England and Great Britain over the years, the pattern of progression has not been the same for professional road and track Black champion cyclists. There has never been a Black rider representing Great Britain at Olympic road or track cycling events. My Made in Britain research work between 2016 and 2022 found that those Black-British cyclists who could have represented Great Britain in track velodrome cycling or on the road at the Olympics had this ambition destroyed by national coaches and selectors. In fact, some were so disillusioned with the system that they gave up the idea of riding for Great Britain at the Olympics of their own accord, feeling that they had no other option than to make enquiries to go back (to their own country) to advance their cycling careers through the countries of their parents' birth. Take Maurice Burton, 1974 British Senior Track Cycling Champion for the 20-kilometre scratch race. He told me:

'Nineteen seventy-six was Olympic year, so I came back to England with the hope that I could come on to the team. So around Easter, I raced in the UK, and I beat them all. I beat the guys. You know, it was an embarrassment. You know, the newspapers were starting to get involved in this. They were asking, "What's going on? How could this guy? Why isn't he even on the squad?" Because there were guys on that squad [who] I don't think had even won a race. So, they had to take me into the squad, and I went through the processes, but I knew pretty much that it wasn't going to work. It wasn't going to happen. I just knew. I could see that some guys fitted, while I didn't. And these were guys who weren't getting the same results in big events like I had been.

'For me, the reason for wanting to go to the Olympic Games was because at that time it was for amateurs, not for professionals. If you could get a good result, then you could turn professional. You could come in on a higher [salary] level. I had to come in at a lower level than those guys, because I didn't have those qualifications. I wanted that qualification, but I couldn't get it. Later on, I did hold a Jamaican passport. What I should have done was gone down that avenue for international racing opportunities.'

But Burton didn't go down that Jamaican avenue. If he had done, he could possibly have been racing at the 1980 Olympic Games in Moscow, Russia, in the same Jamaican team as their track sprint kilometre bronze medal winner, David Weller.

Russell Williams, the 18 times British cycling champion between 1976 and 2002, told me about the chance he had to move away from the UK to race for the USA at the 1984 Olympics and then looking at the possibility to go back to represent his Trinidadian heritage:

'In 1983 and 1984, I was winning big races in the USA. The USA director of cycling said: "I want to pick you for our Olympic team." I said: "Well of course, I can't, being British." At that point, I contacted my father's country of birth, Trinidad and Tobago, and considered riding for them at the 1984 Olympics. But it was difficult with paperwork and letter writing. I guess I left it a bit late as well.'

It seems that Williams held tightly to the hope that the Great Britain cycling team coaches and selectors would call him up. While in his athletic prime, and out of loyalty to being a Black-British man wanting to represent the country of his birth, Williams denied the world stage his presence when he could have represented Trinidad and Tobago and possibly the USA if it could have been made to happen.

There was no hesitation for Christian Lyte, Junior Team Sprint World Champion for Great Britain in 2006 and 2007, and Junior Keirin World Champion in 2006. He told me of how the negativity of his relationships with white British Cycling coaches forced him out of the Great Britain cycling team system. Almost immediately, he made the move to go back and represent his Bajan heritage through the Barbados national track cycling team. He told me:

'I should have been selected [by Great Britain] for more World Cup races. But I didn't get to ride any of those races in Great Britain colours. None. I was never selected. Others were selected and our times on the track were very comparable. I became frustrated. I think at that point I did get in contact with the Barbadian track cyclist Barry Forde via social media.'

Barry Forde had become a national cycling coach for Barbados. Before this, in his racing he had represented Barbados at the UCI World track cycling championships, winning a bronze medal in the Keirin in 2003 and a silver medal in the same event in 2005. The road and track rider Amber Joseph, who is also of British and Bajan heritage, worked with Barry Forde, too. She opted to go back and represent Barbados rather than racing in Great Britain colours. She said to *Cycling Weekly*:

'Barbados has always been my home . . . If I had to choose between England and Barbados . . . Barbados any day. Not just because it's paradise. I find with British Cycling, from the outside and from things that I've heard, it's a little bit more difficult than just riding your bike.'

The road racer Cory Williams, formerly of the USA and now Belize, shared a similar frustration to the Black-British riders when he said:

'I've been one of the top cyclists in America – even the best at my age at one point. I've been national champion, won a stage race overall, won a green jersey, won over 20 state championships and been top 20 at national road races as a junior and never been able to represent America on the national team.'

Williams did finally get a chance to ride for his country of birth, in 2020, when he was selected to represent the USA in the Zwift ESports World Championships. However, in 2022 he followed his brother, the road racer Justin Williams, who in 2021 effectively switched nationalities to go back to ride for the Caribbean island of Belize, the country of his father's birth.

For some Black cyclists born in Western countries like the USA and the UK, to 'go back to your own country' can be to choose to represent your African-Caribbean heritage, relinquishing the default route to the international stage set by your birthplace, which is similar to what white rider, the Kenyan-born Chris Froome did in May 2008 when he removed himself from his national cycling affiliations with the East African country in May 2008. This was so that he could obtain a British racing licence, to give himself the possibility to ride in the 2008 Summer Olympics, as the Kenyan cycling team had failed to qualify. Froome was able to take this opportunity because his parents were born in England. However, the big difference between Froome taking the decision to go back to Great Britain in comparison to Lyte and Joseph giving up their chances of representing Great Britain to represent Barbados is that Froome was returning to a European colonial homeland with huge financial investments in cycling and with opportunities to access leading cycling resources. By cashing in on his white British heritage, Froome went on to win multiple European Grand Tours, thanks to the British support that he received. Whether he could have achieved this level of international success by remaining with Kenya cannot be known, but I doubt it. In contrast, Lyte and Joseph's decision to race for Barbados in my view lessened their chance of possible success on the world stage, because they were compelled to represent a nation without the leading cycling resources and finances compared to Great Britain.

Following in a similar pathway to Lyte and Joseph, the road and track cyclist Red Walters spoke with me about what it meant for him to go back. He was born in England of Grenadian and British parentage. I asked him about shifting from his ambition to represent Great Britain, and what he saw as the possible gains and possible losses in representing Grenada. He said:

'It was something I've been thinking about ever since I started the sport. I've always had both British and Grenadian citizenship. Part of the decision did, of course, come from the opportunities to race internationally. I have also found real joy in representing the other side of my heritage. It's made me even more proud of my roots and my only regret is not switching earlier. To be honest, I don't think there are any major losses. I did look forward to national champs in the UK, but now I'm even more excited about trying to win the Grenadian stripes and representing them in Europe.'

Walters went on to win the Grenadian National Road Race and Individual Time Trial Championships in 2022 and 2023. He also represented Grenada at the 2022 Commonwealth Games in the road and track events. The international stage in cycling is readily available to him via Grenada and it is his choice to brand himself across social media as a recognisable Black professional cyclist wearing the Grenadian National Champion's jersey. But although he is the big fish in the small pool of Grenadian road cycling talent, this also appears to mean that at international events he is generally riding solo as a 'one-man' Grenadian road racing team against world-class riders and teams.

It is France that appears to be the more progressive European nation in terms of Black riders of African or Caribbean heritage making the breakthrough and being accepted as representing their nation's best talent at international level. Over the years many outstanding Black riders have worn the tricolore, including Yavé Cahard. He took silver in the individual sprint at the 1980 Summer Olympics and World Championship cycling medals in 1982, 1983 and 1984. On his shoulders stands Grégory Baugé, the four-time Olympic medallist and nine-time world (individual and team) sprint champion. Taky Marie-Divine Kouamé became the elite women's world sprint champion 500 metre time trial champion in 2022; Melvin Landerneau became European kilometre time trial champion in 2022; and Kévin Reza has represented France in the World Road Race Championships.

Still, Black cyclists from France have not escaped the spectre of racism. During stage 16 of the 2014 Tour de France, Simon MacMichael wrote in *Road.CC* how the Swiss rider Michael Albasini of Orica-Green Edge was accused by Team Europcar manager Jean-René Bernaudeau of calling his rider Kévin Réza a 'dirty negro' when both riders were involved in the break. Albasini insisted he did not make racist comments. During the third stage of the Tour de Romandie in 2017, Réza was racially abused by the Italian rider Gianni Moscon of Team Sky. Moscon admitted this abuse and was suspended for six weeks by Team Sky. When talking about this in *Bicycling*, Réza said that he first thought it wasn't possible that there was still 'that kind of talk' in 2017.

Another incident was the clash between the French rider Nacer Bouhanni and the British rider Jake Stewart during the sprint finish of the Cholet-Pays de la Loire race in March 2021. Stewart avoided crashing his bike and managed to stay upright against the barriers, but unfortunately sustained a broken hand. Bouhanni was disqualified from the race. This led to anger and racism on social media directed at Bouhanni, who is of North African heritage, who was told to 'Go back to Africa!' Some commentators on social media (not Stewart) suggested that the criticism Bouhanni received was because of his lack of contrition about his actions, particularly when he said, 'If he [Jake Stewart] really saw his life flash like he said in that interview, I would advise him to give up sprinting.'

In an interview with L'Équipe TV, Bouhanni accepted his relegation for deviating from his line in the Cholet-Pays de la Loire sprint, but he firmly denied that there had been any malicious intent to harm his fellow rider. Still, a torrent of racist jibes was directed at Bouhanni. On his social media, he wrote:

'Hello to all the little jokers who have been amusing themselves for a week by writing to me personally or commenting on certain cycling websites that I should return to Africa, that I am a criminal, that I am a North African who needs to be interned and who are constantly sending me [pig emoji]. Know that I was born in France and that I am going to file a complaint, because I have been putting up with this for a long time already and I've kept silent, but this time I won't let it go anymore.'

Arguably, Bouhanni's sprinting fouls were not much different to those committed by the Slovakian rider Peter Sagan – a three times World Road Race Champion – who shouldered and headbutted the Belgian rider Wout van Aert at the conclusion of Stage 11 of the 2020 Tour de France late in the sprint to claim second place. And this was not the first time that Sagan had offended. In 2017 the British rider Mark Cavendish was forced out of the Tour de France after suffering a fractured shoulder blade in a serious crash he claimed was caused by Peter Sagan. With both incidents, Sagan faced criticism, but he was not subjected to racial abuse and racial othering about his ethnic identity, with spectators yelling at him or writing on social media 'Go back to Slovakia!'. It seems that only if you are a Black rider or look like you have some African blood in you, with a darker skin pigmentation than European and white riders, that you can be told to 'Go back!'

6

The Biniam BOOM!

At the start of this book, I talked about a 'New Black Cyclone' storming across the world's cycling scene – the incredible Biniam Girmay of Eritrea, who won Gent-Wevelgem in 2022 and became 'the first Black' rider to win a Classic, and then later that same year won stage 10 of the Giro, making him 'the first Black' rider to win a Grand Tour stage. At the 2024 Tour de France, Girmay delivered a hat-trick of sensational sprint victories on stages 3, 8 and 13 of the race. He graced the Green Jersey as the race's best sprinter, winning the competition outright.

My term – the Biniam BOOM! – comes from my interpretation of the heightened cycling media focus and interest concerning Girmay's explosion onto the world's cycling scene. Media headlines from around the world announcing Girmay's 2024 Tour de France stage 3 victory said:

> 'Girmay becomes first Black African to win a Tour de France stage' – *Reuters*
> 'Stage 3: Biniam Girmay Becomes First Black Man in History to Win a Tour de France Stage' – *Bicycling*
> 'Biniam Girmay makes history as first black African to win a Tour de France stage' – *Dereham Times*

'The first Black' has been used as a term by the cycling media seemingly in jubilation of Girmay's extraordinary appearance and the subsequent successes coming with this in the white-dominated world of the sport. 'The first Black' as a headline amplifies Girmay as the new revelation from out of Black Africa. But, as a conscious Black man observing the construction of this narrative, I question the use of 'the first Black' term in a cycling world dominated by whiteness. I do not see the use of this term as giving any genuine cause for Black people's celebration at all. More so, I want to deconstruct the use of the term being absorbed passively without any sense of critical thinking. It is essential to scrutinise the hegemonic power of whiteness in producing hierarchical 'us and them' life comparisons between Black people and white people, and between Black people and those people of other socially constructed groups and racial identities who also see themselves as being above Black people. In my view, 'the first Black' could be implied by those who are using it: 'Black people are so far behind our imagination of modernity, but now look! – Here's one! He's in our world, and he's able to perform and to deliver according to our ways of being and doing.' Interestingly, at the 2024 Tour de France, the EF Education-Easypost rider Richard Capravaz became the first Ecudorian to wear the 'King of the Mountains' jersey. He triumphed outright, winning the title of best climber. But, I did not come across any cycling media headlines that amplified the focus on the colour of his skin, and thus like Girmay, the focus on the dominant norm of white European cyclists in the race.

'The first Black' label in cycling was imposed on Nicholas Dlamini of South Africa for his solitary appearance as a Black rider in the Tour de France in 2021. I thought it was great for Dlamini to be part of a bike race that only a very few racers (Black or white) get the chance to ride in, but I noticed what to me was the curious coincidence of Dlamini's inclusion, which occurred almost at the same time as another Black cyclist – the Frenchman Kévin Reza, who prior to Dlamini's inclusion had ridden multiple Tours de France – announced his retirement from the professional peloton. To me, it looked like one Black face was quickly swapped for another Black face as a tokenistic diversity publicity stunt, particularly following the scrutiny of whiteness given to professional cycling following the Black Lives Matter anti-racism protest by riders at the Tour de France in 2020. I remember watching an early stage of the 2021 Tour de France on television and, as he came to sit down with me, a non-cycling person commented, 'I see that the Black rider from last year is doing well again this year.' I chuckled and turned to him to explain that Kévin Reza had retired from the sport, and it was another Black rider, Nicholas Dlamini, who was racing, but this made me wonder how many once-a-year cycling viewers may have initially thought the same thing. In 2022, there were no Black riders on the Tour de France start list. In 2023 and in 2024, the solitary Black rider at the Tour de France was Biniam Girmay.

In comparison to the appearance of Dlamini and Reza, who are both brilliant Black cyclists, I would say that the Biniam BOOM! became so heightened on Girmay that I began to see in his new white supporters what I would call a 'Desert Orchid fixation' with the man. Desert Orchid was the name of a white racehorse that won several National Hunt Gold Cup races in the UK during the late 1980s and early 1990s, to fanatic public adulation. In these sensational victories the white horse always came ahead of a dominant field of chestnut-brown and dark-coloured horses. It's the other way around in professional cycling racing with Girmay the sole Black man in a field dominated by white riders.

In November 2023, I attended the Rouleur Live event, dubbed 'The world's best cycling show'. This three-day exhibition extravaganza in central London attracted thousands of fans from all over world. They'd come to listen to and meet stage winners of the Giro d'Italia, Tour de France and Vuelta a España. Many of Great Britain's world and Olympic Games cycling champions, and winners of the five European Monuments (the most prestigious one-day races), were in the house. Girmay wasn't there in the flesh, but in his absence he was still being celebrated; at the centre of what I saw as a dominantly white-attended Rouleur Live exhibition was Girmay's image, venerated and distinctively displayed as the focal point of an array of photographs of white cyclists. This instantly reminded me of the 2019 photograph of Nicholas Dlamini at the Tour de Yorkshire in the UK, when he was leading the peloton over Boothferry Bridge during stage 1, in the pouring rain. That photograph went viral and was used as the centre spread of the official programme for the 2019 UCI Road World Championships in Harrogate, Yorkshire. It is an incredible photo by Alex Broadway, ultimately shortlisted for a sports photography award, but I thought part of the reason that it gained so much attention was the sheer novelty of seeing a Black racing cyclist leading the race among a sea of white faces.

There has, of course, been the frenzied support at races that Girmay receives from his native Eritrean fans. Draped in khedra and awlie flags, they sing their songs and chant for him. In this I see the same show of pride in their new national cycling hero as the high-level energy and hype generated around Sir Bradley Wiggins during and for some time after his extraordinary 2012 season of racing, when his huge fan base emerged, seemingly modelled on the England Cricket 'Barmy Army' that travels across the world to their matches and can be seen and heard loudly supporting their team. I remember watching on the Avenue des Champs-Élysées in Paris, on the final day of the 2012 Tour de France. The mock clones of Wiggins were present in their thousands, wearing their stick-on mod sideburns, draped in their union flags, colonising the cafés and the side streets, causing a riot of celebration for their national cycling hero.

Well, the Girmay fans of Eritrea have not gone to such lengths of fanatic parody, but instead some have taken to social media to create fan accounts centred on their 'history-maker'. Whose history? Is Girmay now seen as being a 'history-maker' because of what he has done and achieved so far as 'the first Black' in contributing to the European narrative of cycling's history? If this is the case, then just like the imposition of the term 'the first Black', the term 'history-maker' is also being absorbed and used passively without any sense of critical thinking about the hegemonic power and judgement of the white perspective in reproducing hierarchical 'us and them' life comparisons.

On the weekend of Girmay's Gent-Wevelgem victory in Europe, I was also following another cycling race that was being beamed to my mobile phone from West Africa via Instagram video, so I knew that Moses L Kamara of the Lunsar Cycling Team took the stage 3 victory at the Tour de Lunsar in Sierra Leone. For this, he is also a 'history-maker' in the sport of cycling, but all the global media coverage and attention to cycling is drawn to the magnetic pull of Europe – the centre of the world for cycling and, for many, the only world for cycling of any significance. Gent-Wevelgem is a Classic and Classics are only held in Europe, nowhere else. To be considered at least half-great as a cyclist, you must win one. La Tropicale Amissa Bongo, Tour du Cameroun, Tour de Lunsar, Tour du Rwanda, and all the other races that take place in Africa are not as significant. When Cristián Rodríguez Martin of Spain won the 2021 Tour du Rwanda it didn't make the cycling news headlines and there was no cycling media labelling him as the 'first white' or 'first European'. Spanish cycling fanatics were not crying out 'history-maker' or setting up special social media sites to celebrate and fete the white rider as their new champion.

What would be a wonder to see one day in the future is a European Tour de France winner, who goes on to win the Giro d'Italia and Vuelta a España, and then wins many of the European Classics and Monuments within a few years. It doesn't have to be in that order, but he wins the lot, in his prime. He then calls a press conference to announce to the cycling media and fanatics of the European cycling world of his critical and radical turnabout. As a thought experiment, imagine Tadej Pogačar at age 28 saying:

'Thank you everybody for coming. Right! That's enough of Europe for my career. I have won the big events here in Europe once or twice now and I don't need to repeat myself. I have enough money. My family are fine. I am not coming back. Next year and after that I am going to race in Rwanda with the aim of putting myself on the line with my own team, to win the Tour du Rwanda. The year after, I will travel to Ghana, Burkina Faso and Cameroon hoping to win their best races. Guys! Stop! Think! Europe is just one space for cycling!'

He stands up.

'Why are we so white and Eurocentric about everything in cycling and about us? Why? Tour de France this. Tour de France that. Giro. Vuelta. Guys! The sport of cycling is a big world out there. A pluriverse. Why are we so focused on just us? There is so much out there that I want to experience in my life, especially now, in my professional prime. Not just in Europe. Thank you for your support Goodbye, guys! Goodbye!'

He gets up and walks out of the press conference, to the astonishment of the cycling media.

Of course, this scenario is easier imagined than done. Still, this paradigmatic shift through critical, radical and decolonial thinking put into action for decentring the total focus on Europe is what is needed to create a new wave of seeing and valuing the sport of cycling in its possibilities across the world. And to show that becoming the genuine cycling champion of the people of the world really means going out to create experience and success as a racer to the direct presence and applause of a broader world of cycling people too.

To some extent, it seemed like the multiple European Grand Tour winner Chris Froome was giving recognition to the value of the cycling racing world outside Europe with his appearance at the 2023 Tour du Rwanda. Before the race he said in *Rwanda Today*: 'This is now the 15th edition of the race, which I think speaks volumes to cycling in Rwanda and cycling in Africa. I want to experience that for myself and see the passion for the sport, which I think is growing rapidly in Africa.' Froome was giving some respect to Africa and African cycling, but he was 37 years old, had experienced unfortunate life-changing injuries and it was many years after his wonderful successes in the Grand Tours. Perhaps, Tour de France champions in their prime should be appearing for racing in African countries.

As shown in the earlier chapters of this book, racism towards Black people in cycling was being discussed more openly during and after the Black Lives Matter anti-racism protests across the world in 2020. The multiple sensational victories achieved by Girmay over the last few years in causing the Biniam BOOM! have in my view diverted focus away from underlying issues of racism in cycling that is rooted in whiteness across Europe, North America and Oceania. What about taking action for equity and inclusion of Black people who are born and raised in countries of white-dominated populations that have a history of leadership and success in world cycling? There are possibly thousands of potential Biniam Girmays waiting to be discovered across the UK, Belgium, Italy, Spain, Portugal, Germany, the Netherlands, USA, Canada, New Zealand and Australia. What about their possible development opportunities?

After Girmay's Gent-Wevelgem victory, the former professional triathlete and cyclist Xylon van Eyck told *Velonews:* 'This win is significant because there are so many bike riders [in Africa] watching this who will see a rider like them at the top of the sport, and from today they'll believe that they can do it.' It's wonderful optimism, but we should use history as evidence in other sports to gain some sense of comparison. For example, Tiger Woods of the USA stormed on to the world golf scene to become 'the first Black' man to win a golfing major, the US Masters, in 1997. In the years after this, he won 14 more prestigious golfing majors, but the 'Tiger BOOM!' has not produced an influx of Black champion golfers from across the world to transform the whiteness of the game at the highest levels. Even before this, with professional tennis, how many Black male champions winning major tournaments have we seen since the USA's Arthur Ashe became 'the first Black' to win Wimbledon in 1975? None.

In speaking of Girmay's Gent-Wevelgem victory, the 2020 Giro d'Italia winner, the British rider Tao Geoghegan Hart said, 'This is unbelievable and unreal... I'm shaking from watching that, it's been so incredible.' The British cycling journalist William Fotheringham wrote on social media, 'Wonder if we will look back at today in a few years, maybe five or ten, and see Biniam Girmay's Wevelgem win as a turning point for cycling's spread worldwide, [with a] similar impact to Lucho Herrera's stage win in the 84 Tour. Hope so. Feels like a massive moment.' It is true that since Herrera's victory in 1984, several Colombian riders have showcased to the world their abilities at Grand Tours and in the Classics on a regular basis. With genuine support from leading UCI World Tour teams, Colombian riders such as Egan Bernal have achieved victory at the Tour de France and the Giro d'Italia.

Daniel Teklehaimanot

However, is also true that exceptional talented Black racing cyclists emerging from the African continent have been sharing their capabilities on the UCI World Tour for many years before Biniam Girmay arrived. It's not as if they have just started. The potential power of Eritrean cycling has been represented by Daniel Teklehaimanot, 'the first African' to wear the climbers' polka-dot jersey at the Tour de France, in 2015, and Natnael Berhane, who rode in the event before him. Both riders stand on the shoulders of the foundational cycling legacies of Ghebremariam Ghebru and Weldemichael Asghedom, the original superstars of the Eritrean domestic cycling scene. Then there are Dawit Mehari, Senay Tsegay, Mihretab Kibrab and Habte Weldesimon of the renowned Red Sea Cycling Club that dominated championship cycling in Eritrea between 1994 and 2002.

I discussed what I saw as the hype of the Biniam BOOM! with Dr Robert Child, the Black-British sports scientist, formerly the performance biochemist with Team Katusha and head of nutrition with MTN-Qhubeka. Given his experience working across Africa and coaching Black professional riders, I asked to what extent he saw the emergence of African riders like Girmay as real gamechangers and creating future European Grand Tour winners. He said:

'The African riders have the potential to change riding style in the Grand Tours. Daniel Teklehaimanot had huge powers of recuperation and the ability to cope with high altitude, which were used to get him the Polka Dot jersey. But put those same physical attributes in a climber and we would have a rider who could race in the front group in the mountains every day – with no "easy days" or "truce days" – which would push everyone to the limits and blow the race apart.'

Child's transformational view of potential is tempered to some extent by views given by white South African cycling coach Doug Ryder, former general manager of the Dimension Data team and general manager of Q36.5 Pro Cycling. When speaking to *Velonews* he suggested that some of the Black riders he has worked with couldn't grasp the bigger picture, which reduced their opportunity to shake up representation at World Tour level. He said:

'We had guys who were the pioneers, but there wasn't always that desire to take the next step forward. Daniel [Teklehaimanot] was that guy for a while and he didn't go to the next step. He didn't want to be the total teammate and cycling is a team sport. You go to a Grand Tour and you're only as good as your slowest rider. We had {Ethiopian} Tsgabu Grmay who rode for us for three years and is now on Trek-Segafredo and is doing really well. He left our team because we didn't renew his contract. I think that was a wakeup call for him.' (Curly brackets are author's addition.)

Ryder spoke about his desire to be the one to discover the Black cyclist from Africa who will truly be the sport's changemaker:

'I have always said that I need to find the Michael Jordan of African cycling. Some guy who will go deep into his career and continue to improve. I haven't found him yet. When I look at Amanuel [Ghebreigzabhier] {of Eritrea}, he may be it. He has a different glint in his eye. There's a fire that burns deep inside him like he has a flame that he doesn't want to let go. Maybe he's going to be something special. We need a guy who competes at the top consistently and doesn't say, "This is just a job."' (Curly brackets are author's addition.)

Ryder's desire is clear. Still, maybe whatever 'the top' means perhaps requires a deeper and broader rethinking outside white and Eurocentric ideals. There seem to be differing ethnic and cultural perspectives for this, given the broken partnerships that Ryder has experienced with some of the fantastic Black riders that have worked with him.

Nonetheless, interpreting the meaning of 'the top' didn't apply to understanding the 'New Black Cyclone', Biniam Girmay. Before the 2023 Tour de France began I knew how much anticipation of victory there was for him, because I had already been contacted by three cycling media outlets asking me to be ready to write about Girmay being 'the first Black' rider from Africa to take a stage victory at the Tour. All cycling media outlets that contacted me seemed to be convinced this would happen. The headline of one article on the BBC Sport website read, 'Tour de France: Biniam Girmay is leading a revolution in cycling', but responses on social media to this claim pointed out there had been many African riders in the peloton over the years, including Chris Froome, Daryl Impey, Robbie Hunter and Louis Meintjes, and they had won Grand Tour stages.

The way I saw it, the article was about racism in cycling over the years, albeit indirectly, and about the emergence of Girmay in being an indigenous and Black African cyclist coming into a world dominated by white European cyclists. For me, the interesting point in the social media comments was about the white riders being 'African', because they may have been born in Africa but that is always going to be a debate about African indigeneity and ethnogenesis, particularly when considering their dominant European ethnic group origins.

The 2023 Tour de France media hype around Girmay was to be expected following his explosion as the 'New Black Cyclone' storming the world cycling scene. No doubt, some cycling writers had fully drafted their 2023 Tour de France accounts of his life story and had them oven-ready for dishing out to their readership immediately after they had seen 'the first Black' rider win a Tour de France stage race, but it didn't happen. The closest Girmay came was on the race into Bordeaux on 7 July, where he finished third after the eventual stage winner, the Belgian sprinter Jasper Philipsen, deviated from the line. Girmay's Intermarché–Circus–Wanty team appealed against Philipsen's deviation, but this was turned down, and the result stood. The cycling and social media hype died down and when people realised Girmay wasn't going to deliver the 'history-maker' story it created a flat ending to his 2023 Tour de France. Following this, Girmay suffered injuries in a crash at the Clásica de San Sebastián, which made him a non-starter for the UCI Road World Championships in Scotland in August 2023. But at the 2024 Tour de France the world witnessed Girmay's transfiguration. All disappointments in expectation of success during the previous year were erased.

The cycling media discourses fuelling what I have defined as the Biniam BOOM! present Girmay as the revolutionary 'New Black Cyclone' from Africa – storming the white-dominated world of the sport. Following his maiden victory at the 2024 Tour de France, Girmay wrote on his social media accounts, 'Let me open the door'. For me, this came across as a messiah-like communication, giving to oppressed Black people all over the world the message that the deliverer had finally arrived to actualise all hopes of passage into heaven. With the 2025 UCI World road race championships set to take place for the first time in Africa – in Kigali, Rwanda – the amplification across the world of Girmay's words and his image as the 'New Black Cyclone' out of Africa serves to fulfil the motivation of an 'interest-convergence'. In this communication of hope, Girmay – the 'New Black Cyclone' – is elevated as the aspirational figure, just like the original Black Cyclone Major Taylor (Jesus Christ of the Black cycling community in the USA). Aspirant cyclists who share in Girmay's image will use his invitation as a solid reference point for their hopes and dreams of a life in European professional cycling.

7

Representing the entire human race of Black women

The 2022 Commonwealth Games Road Races were being held in Birmingham, England. I had met and spoken with some of the African and Caribbean cyclists from across these Commonwealth-affiliated nations who were going to be competing in the race. Unfortunately, I was unable to visit the event as a spectator, so I watched on television at home. As I flicked through the channels in search of the BBC TV coverage, I paused when I saw that the Hollywood film *Gone with the Wind*, made in

1939, was being screened as a Sunday matinee. This film brought to mind some interesting comparisons with the world of professional cycling.

I could compare ethnic representation in professional cycling on the UCI World Tour today to the ethnic representation in some of those Hollywood movies of the 1930s and 1940s. Both worlds are dominated by whiteness, and both worlds heap adulation and superstar status on their leading performers. Yes, from time to time the odd Black actor appears in some of those old movies, albeit as the mammy, the butler or the chauffeur, serving white people. And yes, over the past 10 years or so Black riders have ridden the Tour de France and the Tour de France Femmes, but it is extremely rare if they are in leading roles. However, the similarity ends with present-day Hollywood: the dominance of white actors in leading movie roles has shifted and more Black stars headline Hollywood films: Will Smith, Denzel Washington, Samuel L Jackson, Eddie Murphy, Morgan Freeman, Viola Davis, Jada Pinkett Smith, Lupita Nyong'o – this is a non-exhaustive list. By contrast, the white dominance on the UCI World Tour races, for men and women, remains stuck in a 1930s and 1940s Hollywood time warp.

Whether you agree with my 'old' Hollywood analogy or not, the facts of the two white-dominated worlds remain. The lives of generation after generation of Black people from the USA and across Europe are rooted in the poisonous racism of transatlantic slavery. Black people in this Western world are also framed by the realities of a dominant Eurocentric imagination and by waking up every day to the narrative of this. The world of professional cycling is definitely no exception.

When thinking about the numerical presence of Black female professional racing cyclists, it is fair to say that they are rare and totally underrepresented across all the disciplines on the world stage of cycling at world-class level in comparison to white female cyclists. Yes, a few notable and outstanding Black female cyclists have emerged, but only more recently: Teniel Campbell, the road racing cyclist from Trinidad and Tobago; Taky Marie-Divine Kouamé of France, the 2022 World Champion in the 500-metre time trial; and former Black-British world BMX champion Shanaze Reade. Kadeena Cox is also well known in the UK through her successes as a Paralympian athlete and the Dominican-born Dutch rider, Ceylin del Carmen Alvarado, has won numerous cyclo-cross World Cup events, and European and World Championship titles. These are riders as outstanding individuals who can be seen as leading lights in their representation of Black women in cycling. However, it is fair to point out that there have never been two or three Shanaze Reades, Kadeena Coxes or Ceylin del Carmen Alvarados dominating racing across their respective cycling disciplines at the same time in the same world-leading events, particularly in comparison to the number of white female cyclists who participate. Individually, when Reade, Cox and del Carmen Alvarado, and all those mentioned above, take to the world stage of cycling, for me it is like each of them is representing all Black women of the human race.

In 2021, the Eritrean road cyclist Mosana Debesay became more widely known in connection with the beginning of African women's participation in the Olympic Games. She said: 'I know I'm representing the whole continent of Africa and that every African is going to support me, which is filling me with excitement.' By the 'whole continent of Africa' what Debesay is referring to is Black people in Africa. By 'every African' what I interpret that as meaning, in effect, is Black people all over the world.

Celebratory discourses given to Debesay – as 'the first African' to represent Black women at the Olympics are complicit in validating and reproducing power and status given to the Western [white] construct. Originating in 1896 by the concept of European aristocrats in their notions of Enlightenment and 19th-century 'progress' worldviews, the modern Olympic Games has grown as a mega-event of global reach. Non-Western nations have been influenced to join and follow this grand Eurocentric narrative as a route to salvation from their non-Western ways of being. Use of terms such as 'the first Black' man and 'history-maker' applied to Biniam Girmay as discussed in the previous chapter, and phrases such as 'the first Black' woman applied to Debesay's story, communicate that Black people are only now, in the third decade of the 21st century, beginning to live by their access to the light of the Western [white] world's imagination and spirit.

The cyclist Ayesha McGowan of the USA was correct in describing cycling as being possibly the whitest sport on Earth. She saw it as her personal mission to change this and in 2021 she signed to race for Liv Racing on the UCI World Tour, albeit as a stagiaire – a trainee professional rider – at the age of 35. All of this came in the aftermath of Black Lives Matter and perhaps some observers would think that Liv Racing was using McGowan to show ethnic diversity in its brand and bike products. However, others would say that by developing this partnership with Liv Racing, McGowan provided a visual representation of a determined Black woman in action in professional cycling at World Tour level during the latter part of that racing season. I wonder how things would have panned out for McGowan if she had been able to do that at, say, age 23.

One way the experience of a young Black woman from outside Europe in their early twenties making an entry to the world stage and experiencing the UCI World Tour for cycling can be seen is through Teniel Campbell of Trinidad and Tobago. The saying 'Luck is when an opportunity comes along and you're prepared for it' appears to have held true for Campbell, as she recounts: 'I had a golden opportunity in 2017 to travel to Martinique for the Caribbean Cycling Championships. While I was there, I met UCI president David Lappartient after I won double gold, and he was very impressed and invited me to the UCI Training Centre in Switzerland.'

From there, Campbell signed with the Australian professional cycling team, Mitchelton-Scott. Campbell was the beginning of Black female representation on the UCI Women's World Tour and positioned in a white-dominated space among the biggest female road cycling star performers of the sport and had the chance to develop into a huge and unique cycling superstar herself. However, one of Campbell's initial experiences as a young Black woman was the frosty reaction she received from her new white peers. She said: 'I never paid attention to my skin colour or anyone else's. For me, it is important that someone sees my potential and not the colour of my skin. But I do remember arriving at my first professional races in Norway and noticing from people's facial reactions how surprised they were to see me.'

My 1930s and 1940s Hollywood time warp parallel comes to the fore again. I can juxtapose Campbell's experience with the racial othering experienced by the Hollywood actor Hattie McDaniel. She is widely remembered for her Oscar-winning performance as the Mammy in *Gone with the Wind*. Still, before this award, she experienced detestable reactions to her Blackness from white people. McDaniel was unable to attend the film premiere in Atlanta in 1939, because it was held at a whites-only theatre, and at the Academy Awards ceremony in Los Angeles the following year where she was to receive her award, she was forced to sit apart in a segregated area at the side of the room. This makes me think of another Oscar-winning Black female actor, Halle Berry, who said, 'I am not implying that Hollywood is racist, but racism is so subtle that people sometimes won't even realise . . . I don't have to try to be accepted. I have to try to get people to have more tolerance and accept me as I am. I am not the one that needs to change.' Teniel Campbell was made to question her Black skin in the presence of white people, but in Berry's words it is not Campbell that 'needs to change', but, if it truly wants to embrace the global ethnic diversity of top cyclists, it is the white cycling world around her that must change.

Teniel Campbell

Perhaps to be seen and known as representing the entire human race of Black women in the white-dominated world of cycling can provide a unique and powerful opportunity to blaze a trail as a leader, to create the pathway for more Black females to follow, but this opportunity can become a heavy burden to carry, as the 2022 Canyon-SRAM Generation rider, Jamaican Llori Sharpe, explained to me:

'At times I certainly feel like I stand out like a sore thumb, but it provides me with the opportunity to showcase the talent that can come from the Caribbean region. However, that feeling of being a sole representative for a country, region and/or race can sometimes be extremely pressuring, overwhelming and a bit burdensome, especially when I don't perform as well as I would've liked and thoughts of not being good enough or not representing well enter my mind.'

Llori's 2022 Canyon-SRAM Generation Rwandan teammate, Valentine Nzayisenga, also appeared to recognise the challenge faced by Black women cycling at the top level. She told me: 'I love cycling because I started it in 2017. The effect is that when I perform in a race, I look at the write-up in cycling reports, and whatever this says, it makes me work harder, to show it to us as Black people, we can.' To what extent are Campbell and McGowan causing mindsets and norms of thinking about the presence of Black women in the sport, and in road racing in particular, to change? It will be interesting to see what the impact of having the likes of Teniel Campbell and Ayesha McGowan as Black women racing and representing all Black women on the UCI World Tour will be 10 years from now.

One of the immediate outcomes for grassroots development was through McGowan's Thee Abundance Mini-Grant. This financial funding enabled nine Black women to participate in the Tour of America's Dairyland (TOAD), which was held from 17–21 June 2021 in communities throughout southeast Wisconsin. In 2022, the Thee Abundance Mini-Grant funding was extended to provide entries, housing, transportation, a food stipend and several additional resources for awardees for four major road races – the Tulsa Tough, Tour of America's Dairyland, Intelligentsia Cup and Gateway Cup. This leadership from McGowan gave Black women across the USA an opportunity to form teams or to network to collectively pursue their ambitions in racing. However, one of the beneficiaries, Ajoa Abrokwa from Philadelphia, told me how even though the opportunity was positive, it also further raised her awareness of the hostility and 'whiteness of the sport and racism encountered by Black people.'

For Llori Sharpe, the representation given by Campbell and McGowan has been important for her own sense of belonging and ambition in World Tour racing:

'My desire to ride competitively and aim for the professional rankings was undoubtedly inspired by my fellow Caribbean cyclist Teniel

Campbell. Seeing her and how she has progressed in the World Tour scene encouraged me to pursue professional cycling. Representation is extremely important as it fosters feelings of inclusivity, as well as one's perception of something. If you don't see people who look, act or have similar life experiences, you'll probably feel like an outsider, but having those familiar faces contributes to feelings of inclusion and belongingness in a community.'

The influential presence of Campbell as a Black woman racing on the World Tour can be seen through the rise of the USA racer Sheerie Edwards. She became the Florida State Criterium Champion in 2022, even though she had only begun road cycling during the COVID-19 pandemic. She told me:

'I really didn't have any inspiration beyond keeping the quarantine pounds at a minimum. Racing wasn't in mind then either. But, as I grew into the sport, started to watch videos from USA Crits, now called National Criterium Series, and made friends within the local cycling community, that's when I discovered Teniel Campbell. They would often sing praises about her talent and prowess on the bike. That's who I saw as a representation of where I could be granted to move toward the competitive side of cycling. When Teniel placed first overall in stage 6 of the 2021 Tour Cycliste Féminin International de l'Ardèche, her followers/supporters on Instagram and other social media platforms went crazy. It was so great to witness. I'm sure she gained a couple thousand followers after that win.'

But is the representation of one or two Black female cyclists on the UCI World Tour of any impact, even if they are not winning regularly? According to Edwards, it is:

'Black people will root for everyone Black and support the culture. Take a look at dominant athletes from other sports, such as Tiger Woods, Serena and Venus Williams, for example. Black people in America were not well represented in the sport of golf and tennis before these giants came along. It sparked the interest in the Black community and gave young boys and girls exposure, and a sense of opportunity to try a new sport and become the next legend.'

Perhaps the next legendary Black woman cyclist may come through the developmental work of the Germany-based Canyon-SRAM Generation team. Over the years they have provided international racing contracts for Black female cyclists such as Olivia Shililifa, the 2021 Under-23 Road Race Champion of Namibia, Valentine Nzayisenga of Rwanda, and Llori Sharpe of Jamaica. In 2023, Diane Ingabire of Rwanda was recruited to the squad. In 2024, Ese Lovina Ukpeseraye, the 2023 African Continental Road Race Champion, joined them, as did the Ugandan road racer, Florence Nakagwa. From what I know, these are generally one-year racing contracts and, while on the surface this may seem to be shaping global multi-ethnic representation at World Tour level, Llori Sharpe gives a pragmatic response:

'Admittedly, the representation of a few Black female cyclists may not be enough, but it's a start. Moreover, if more teams such as Canyon-SRAM make a deliberate attempt to provide opportunities for the underrepresented, the growth of Black cyclists in the World Tour (whether female or male) will ensue. As it relates to winning, dominating and achieving top placements, those are undoubtedly encouraging to attract people, but it is the retention of those cyclists that'll foster changed attitudes.'

Sharpe also suggests that there is still some way to go at grassroots level, for example in Jamaica, for genuine growth in the representation of Black women on the World Tour to happen:

'Cycling's popularity hasn't been where it should be in Jamaica for quite a while. For girls and women specifically, it's even less popular, but I must say that there has been some progress given the increase in numbers of junior girls taking on the sport. I'd say a huge hindrance to cycling's popularity is that it's relatively less accessible than other sports in Jamaica, such as track and field, netball, football etc. Not only are these other sports embedded in our schooling system at the primary, secondary and tertiary levels, but they are also less costly from a participative and administrative standpoint. However, some progress has been made, but there's still a lot more work that needs to be done.'

Llori Sharpe

Jamaica has a historical point of reference for producing champion cyclists, particularly the 1980 Olympic sprint cycling medallist David Weller, but no female cycling champions come to mind, not even sprinters. This is stark when compared to Jamaica's historical successes with female track and field sprinters.

I switched the television channel and found the 2022 Commonwealth Games' women's road race. There were 32 kilometres to go, and the commentator was talking about the breakaway, the group of riders out in front, and the presence of riders from key nations. I saw the white riders in their national jerseys of Australia, Canada, Scotland and Wales, and wondered what the commentator meant by key nations, because also very present in the leading group was the unmissable presence and riding style of Teniel Campbell, representing her one-woman racing team of Trinidad and Tobago.

The race continued, and the BBC TV pictures screened the wonderful rolling lanes of the English countryside surrounding Warwick Castle.

However, to the frustration of the commentators, it wasn't the leading group that managed to break up the race, but errors in the BBC TV transmission and reception that caused a fizzling across my TV screen, and coverage of the racing was lost for a short period. When a clear TV screen returned, the riders were heading towards a sprint finish. The Australian team took control of lead-out, with the aim of delivering their rider Georgia Baker to the line, as others hustled for position. At 500 metres out Campbell was still present and looking very intent on finishing with a flurry. At one point she almost hit the barrier, trying to sneak through a gap that maybe wasn't there. Then she found herself in the centre of the bunch, third row back and boxed in. Could she do it? At 200 metres out, she was looking for space with no specific wheel to follow. At 100 metres out she simply had no space. Game over! The win was taken by Baker of Australia, guided home by a well-organised and efficient lead-out, including her teammate Sarah Roy, who took third place. Teniel was just a couple of bike lengths behind in sixth place, which was an extremely respectable result for a Commonwealth Games road race in a field of that calibre.

For me, I imagined the race ending differently. In my mind, I saw a full team of female riders from Trinidad and Tobago, including three powerful riders in the image of Campbell, working for their leader, a sprint train riding flat out, heading for the finish line. The result – gold for Campbell.

8

Visiting Velokhaya

Before and during the 2023 UCI World Cycling Championships in Glasgow, I saw how the national cycling federation for South Africa – Cycling South Africa – were very active on social media, continually posting fine words of support alongside photographs of their participating riders. One of the Cycling South Africa's social media posts proudly announced:

'The Elite Men's Team representing South Africa in the Road Race and Time Trial: Daryl Impey, Ryan Gibbons, Callum Ormiston, Morne Van Niekerk.'

Another post from Cycling South Africa read:

'Today's the day! Let's rally behind our incredible Paracycling champs, Pieter du Preez and Goldy Fuchs, as they hit the road in pursuit of victory. Show them your support. Go for gold, Pieter and Goldy!'

Cycling South Africa even posted support and celebration of their participants in the amateur categories:

'We're so proud of our #TEAMSA Grandfondo riders who are ready to take on the roads of Scotland in the Grandfondo UCI World Championships.
    'The race will start and finish in the beautiful city of Perth. Wishing riders the best of luck!!'

What I observed about the elite men's team and the paracyclists, alongside all 13 Grandfondo riders pictured on the Cycling South Africa posts, was that they were all white cyclists. This was not something new for me to see. Over the years I had observed representation in South African teams in cycling across most disciplines of the sport, but particularly in Grand Tour road racing, World Championships and Commonwealth Games events have always been totally dominated by white cyclists. Given that the white people of South Africa have always been a minority group compared to the majority Black people, the ethnic dominance of whiteness in representing South Africa in cycling on the world stage has always been curious to me.

South Africa's 2022 census showed Black people as the dominant population group at 81.4 per cent, followed by the Coloured population at 8.2 per cent. The percentage of white people named on the census had declined to 7.3 per cent in 2022, from 8.9 per cent in 2011, while the population of Indians or Asians within the Coloured population named on the census had increased slightly, from 2.5 per cent in 2011 to 2.7 per cent in 2022.

Prior to looking at these numbers, and during the public dissemination of my Made in Britain cycling research, I received an extraordinarily powerfully written email from South Africa, of which the signatories have asked to remain unnamed. Here is a part of it:

'Dear Dr Moncrieffe,
We're reaching out to discuss racism in cycling. The background to this request is this: South Africa needs to reform its cycling institutions. We've experienced and witnessed racism in South Africa (no surprise there), but specifically in cycling. We have been targeted by other organisations and the official cycling federation, Cycling South Africa, have dismissed any claims of racism against their commissaires that we've tabled over the years. We've been gaslit and treated as "the troublemakers" when we call out racism.'

In 1994, Apartheid 'formally' came to an end in South Africa. However, the trauma of racial violence inflicted on Black people during those ugly years appears to continue for some. No doubt, post-Apartheid trauma may have been experienced by the white minority population of South Africa too, particularly through having to adapt to the reality of being among a transformed and dominant Black majority in power and in leadership of the nation. To provide a detailed understanding of living standards in South Africa with a focus on social and economic inequities framed by race and ethnic group categories, in 2022 the World Bank published a report which stated, 'South Africa . . . is the most unequal country in the world, ranking first among 164 countries . . . race remains a key driver of high inequality, due to its impact on education and the labor market . . . The legacy of colonialism and Apartheid, rooted in racial and spatial segregation, continues to reinforce inequality.' Racial inequities are embedded in South Africa and the monster of Apartheid continues to haunt economic, social and sporting contexts, including cycling.

I made contact with Arnold Sibanda, a Black community cycling leader based in Johannesburg. We'd been following each other on social media. I wanted to gain his impressions of cycling for Black people in the past, compared to the present in South Africa. He told me:

'Cycling was generally inaccessible to Black people during Apartheid; even owning a bicycle wasn't as easy as it is today. Bicycles were status symbols for the wealthy to tour around and to use for sport. White cycling associations were created to "gatekeep" cycling. The mining aristocracy, known as the Rand Pioneers, pushed in 1905 for a city-wide rule mandating that Black riders wear a badge on their left arm as proof of council authorization. It was even claimed that any natives on bicycles had probably stolen them or, if not, rode them dangerously, so they had to be policed and monitored. Black cyclists were totally subjected to a system of racial segregation and discrimination. Looking at competitive cycling since Apartheid, there have been developments in the sport, in that we've seen a number of Black people in competitive races nationally, but very few internationally. Work is needed here, and we still need to see more development programmes at grassroots level and in disadvantaged communities, such as rural areas and townships.'

Arnold's response, and the email that was sent to me, further fuelled my curiosity. They made me want to learn more about the stories given by Black people of South Africa in cycling. Why is it that white cyclists dominate the South African international scene?

My first understanding of South Africa when I was younger came from the television news. This generally gave lots of airtime to the social troubles caused by Apartheid – a racist system of national governance which provided greater social and life privileges to the minority colonial migrant white people over the multiple indigenous majority ethnic groups of Black people. The television images were of large groups of Black people marching together, bouncing up and down, singing and chanting for equal rights and the dismantling of the Apartheid system. I once saw how the mass group of Black people did this, approaching a wall of white South African police who were using their vehicles as a barricade to the oncoming force. As the tension grew, the police would fire water cannons to extinguish the public protest. Then, as the television journalist paused, cracking sounds of gunfire and the angry barking of dogs could be heard, as the singing and chanting of the protestors morphed into screams and cries. I saw protestors fleeing for their lives, running in different directions, not all escaping without harm. To me, the television coverage of the late 1980s and early 1990s anti-Apartheid protests in South Africa often made it look as though Black people were the troublemakers. Well, of course they were! This was a just troublemaking to challenge the colonial power of the unjust troublemakers of the racist Apartheid system that had been oppressing and killing Black people for decades.

Another incident was at secondary school, and I remember being ushered by teachers into the television room to watch the film *Cry Freedom*, the 1987 epic Apartheid drama set in late-1970s South Africa. The name of the Black consciousness leader Steve Biko stayed with me. I understood that there were white people who were anti-Apartheid and some white friends helped him escape in a small plane to a place called Lesotho. The fact that he was a Black man who spoke out against white government oppression, and that the police wanted to arrest him and kill him because of this, all connected to the reality of my youth, too, although the teachers at my secondary school didn't connect what was happening in South Africa to what was happening in the UK. This was the racism I had witnessed first-hand with my family, most of whom lived in Brixton, southwest London, and were caught up in the uprisings of 1981 and 1985. This was a time of everyday Metropolitan police violence towards Black people, including multiple deaths of Black people in police custody. Our Black Lives Matter responses to the oppressive white racist system, including our struggles with the Metropolitan Police and Margaret Thatcher's Conservative government, were similar in some ways to the struggles occurring in South Africa.

I found out more about South African culture in the final year of secondary school, when a white friend asked me and another white friend to work with him in his father's butcher's shop. As far as I know, he and his father were not from South Africa, but they owned this specialist butcher's shop that prepared and sold beef biltong, a South African delicacy. It was a strange environment. From what I remember, the only customers were white people from South Africa, but my friend and I didn't get involved with serving them. We stayed in the back, out of the way, preparing the seasoning sauces for the slabs of beef biltong and making the sausages, but even above the music on the radio we could often hear the customers talking away loudly at each other, mixing English and Afrikaans in their excitement at seeing the numerous beef biltong joints that were hung up to dry around the shop, the sausages and the stacks of Castle Lager that were on display.

I left that job in February 1990, around the same time as the anti-Apartheid leader Nelson Rolihlahla Mandela, the co-founder of uMkhonto we Sizwe, a militant wing of the South African political party, the African National Congress, was released from his 27 years of imprisonment by the white South African government, thus making it possible for *all* South African people to be released from their Apartheid prison.

During the Apartheid years, there were in fact some very active non-segregated competitive cycling races between Black and white cyclists. As the writer Geoff Waters discusses in his article, competitive cycling organised by the mine workers on the South African gold mines from the late 1950s to the mid-1980s was led by Black people and was for Black cyclists only, because of Apartheid. However, these events grew hugely in popularity, causing local white cyclists to break their own laws of racial segregation to participate. The champion Black cyclists from these gold mines included the likes of John Moding, Pefeni Mtembu, Siphiwe Ngwenya, Jack Ntseou (of Botswana) and Elias Ramantele.

The racist Apartheid government regime was facing increased criticism from around the world. Sanctions against the country were being imposed. This meant that South Africa was excluded from the 1964 Olympic Games and in 1970, the South African Cycling Federation (SACF) was suspended by the UCI. South African cyclists were prevented from participating in UCI meetings abroad, so the SACF needed to engage with the Black cycling community in the gold mines in order to generate competitive fields for its own events.

Black and white cyclists competed as separate teams at the 1973 Rapport Toer, an international race held around Cape Town. That year three foreign teams took part, contravening their own governments' bans on participation in South African sporting events. The one team of Black cyclists at the race was called Clover. This consisted of the mine workers

John Moding, Richard Moteka, Abie Oromeng and Elias Ramatele. It was Moding who shone the brightest in the race. At the end of the event, he shared victory in the overall King of the Mountains classification with Mike Carey, a white cyclist from South Africa. In later years, the Black cyclists from the gold mines continued to form as teams for racing at the Rapport Toer, matching and beating the best of the white professional riders from South Africa and the 'rebel' European professionals too. For example, Jack Ntseou took an outstanding solo stage victory during the 1979 version of the Rapport Toer.

Following Mandela's release from prison in 1990, the international embargo on South African professional sporting competitions, including cycling, was lifted, but it was a staggering 18 years until the first Black cyclist represented South Africa at international level, with BMX rider Sifiso Nhlapo competing at the 2008 Olympic Games in Beijing, China, and at the London Olympics in 2012. It took even longer for Black South African road racers to emerge on to the world stage.

In 2015, some 25 years after the international embargo was lifted, Songezo Jim, a Black cyclist from South Africa, appeared for Team Pro-Touch at the Vuelta a España, and then for Team Pro-Touch at the 2016 Giro d'Italia. Following in Jim's footsteps, Nicholas Dlamini won the King of the Mountains classification in the Tour of Britain and Australian Tour Down Under in 2018. Dlamini represented South Africa at the 2021 Olympic Games, and he rode in the 2021 Tour de France for the team Qhubeka-NextHash.

Songezo Jim

However, Dlamini's success did not come without some extremely sad moments. In 2019, while out training on his road bike, he had his arm broken during a violent assault by park ranger guards at the Table Mountain National Park in Cape Town. On stage 9 of the 2021 Tour de France, he crashed early on and finally crossed the line over one hour behind the stage winner after an isolated ride in the cold and the rain – it was tough viewing for all his fans. For all the talk of the ancient African 'ubuntu' solidarity term as 'I am what I am because of who we are' as a key value in his team Qhubeka NextHash, his ride was a very public, lonely effort, with no teammate around to support him. To me, it seemed almost as if he was being left out there alone to be shamed. He was eliminated from the race and, although he took this well and spoke gracefully about his love of being in the Tour de France, it was in sharp contrast to the fervent celebrations of joy across the cycling world just days earlier about Dlamini becoming 'the first Black' rider from South Africa to race in the event.

Following their appearances across the three Grand Tours, both Jim and Dlamini were unable to sustain their relatively short presence on the UCI World Tour road racing scene, this in comparison to white South African riders such as Daryl Impey, Louis Meintjes and Ryan Gibbons. All have enjoyed lengthier and successful experiences at this level, and across a variety of World Tour teams too. White sanction – an exclusive endorsement given to Black people from the white people who hold the power of enablement for allowing access and possible advancement in the sport – gave Jim and Dlamini as Black riders from South Africa the opportunity to race across the Grand Tours. It may be debatable whether this was a tokenistic sanction or was genuinely fuelled by a motive to challenge the status quo, the systems and structures of racism at UCI World Tour levels by non-representation of Black cyclists across the teams. But, the fact is, both Jim and Dlamini did not last long, and not many riders like them from South Africa have followed. Still, a couple of sentences can now be written into the Eurocentric cycling histories about Jim and Dlamini becoming 'the first' of their kind (Black riders) from South Africa in giving representation to their people in cycling's Grand Tours. This seems to me as though now the Black man has been taken to the moon, there is no need to take that Black man there again, there is no need to repeat the mission. The 'diversity box' has been ticked. This may be the attitude. Certainly, Dlamini was clearly concerned about the absence of Black riders in the 2022 Tour de France when he told *Cycling Weekly* that it was 'disturbing' that the 'biggest cycling event in the world' still had no Black riders in the peloton. He found it a 'disappointment and a huge step back'.

Nicholas Dlamini

The Velokhaya Life Cycling Academy of Cape Town was key to nurturing Dlamini during the early years of his cycling adventures. The name 'Velokhaya' is derived from two words – the French word for cycling (vélo) and the Xhosa word for home (khaya) – so it translates as 'home of the bicycle'. When I travelled to South Africa for Visting Velokhaya, I wanted to learn as much as I could about the work that they do in their community; to share some stories from my book, *Desire, Discrimination, Determination*; to welcome school sports teachers and community leaders from the Western Province of South Africa to the cycling for schools coaching project that I had devised for advancement of curriculum teaching and learning with young children; and I definitely wanted to make time to go out for a ride with the Velokhaya guys to explore some parts of Cape Town.

I arrived in Cape Town and got a taxi to the hotel in the Century City area. This was a last-minute booking with a huge discount, but I guess I had misread things as it wasn't in the centre of the city, but on the outskirts, and Century City was not what I had expected. I was staying in a commercial shopping area with high-profile retailers, and Porsche and Mercedes car dealerships, all located opposite the magnificent and iconic Table Mountain.

My next day in Cape Town was a total contrast. I travelled by taxi to the Khayelitsha township where the Velokhaya Life Cycling Academy is based. Townships came about under the racist Apartheid regime when, in 1950, the Group Areas Act designated land across the country for the sole use of specific racial groups. This meant that Black people were evicted from their homes and properties and forced to move into racially segregated townships across South Africa – the name 'Khayelitsha' is the Xhosa word for 'new home'. What I saw there was a multiplicity of clustered corrugated-aluminium shacks. People were washing their clothes in basins outside their homes and others were chopping raw meat on tables outside. Smoky fires were burning in barrels on street corners, while 20 kilometres or so away in gift-wrapped Century City there were fast-food outlets, restaurants and cinemas. I could compare Khayelitsha to Trench Town in Kingston, Jamaica. I'd been through there on a couple of occasions. This was a notoriously dangerous place, renowned for gang warfare, drugs, killings and murders, particularly during the 1970s and 1980s. Somehow, Khayelitsha gave me the sense that it had been through similar troubles to those experienced in Trench Town, rooted in government neglect of a people in need, resulting in their impoverished, under-resourced state.

I found the gem of the Velokhaya Life Cycling Academy within the township, but I noticed the ominous ringed barbed wire running across the high boundary fencing of the site. A gateman pulled at an opening to let us into the small car park. This was situated next to a wonderfully colourful modern brick building. The space had a BMX track with jumps and berms. This seemed the ideal place for young people to escape into another world, an oasis amidst their township.

I met the manager of Velokhaya Life Cycling Academy, Sipho Mona, a former elite BMX rider. He walked me around the facility. There was pride in his voice as he spoke about the development of the academy, and the use of cycling and education to empower young people to see the possibility of greater life opportunities outside their township. The entrance foyer of the academy was decorated with trophies and framed photographs of teams gone by. There was a classroom so young, members of the academy could carry out their school homework. There was a mechanics room with cycling tools spread across worktops. There was even a room that housed a few Wattbikes, although these seemed in need of upgrading.

As we walked and talked, Sipho told me that he got into cycling through his uncle, who had formed a social club for the sport in the early 1990s. I asked him whether things had got better or worse for Black people and Black-led cycling clubs since the end of Apartheid, and he said, 'Well, a lot relies on the position or wealth of your family. It is pretty much like motorsport racing or golf where you need a lot of support financially to make it to the international foundational circuit. We [Black people] can only do the best that we can to mitigate that gap.'

Based on what I had learned about the very apparent social and economic inequities across South Africa, and the gulf between the wealthy minority white people and the majority Black people who are generally less wealthy, making it to the 'international foundational circuit' is very much loaded in favour of South Africa's wealthy minority white population.

Sipho introduced me to his colleague, Litha Mbadlisa, the head coach for cycling development and himself an elite road-racing cyclist. Litha told me that he was born and raised in the Khayelitsha township and had come through Velokhaya's cycling and education support system. He told me that he got into the sport in 2007, when some of his friends came through the section of the township where he lived riding their bikes and wearing Velokhaya cycling kits. From that moment, he knew he had to find out how he could join the academy. He told me:

'Growing up in the township, 90 per cent of people didn't know cycling as a sport, they only saw a group of boys riding bikes around. That's all. Then Luthando Kaka came to light. Yes, Luthando Kaka was the most promising young talent within Black cycling in Cape Town. This is when the original cycling team formed, named as the Millennium

Life Cycling Academy, then years later turning into the Velokhaya Life Cycling Academy.'

I asked Litha the same question – Had things got better or worse for Black cyclists and Black-led clubs since the 'formal' end of Apartheid? – and he said, 'Things got better when Black riders were able to be selected by more resourced teams, but things have got worse with cycling equipment being so much more expensive for Black-led clubs to afford.'

We took a walk outside, towards the BMX track. We climbed the stairs to the start gate, where we had an elevated view of the venue. I could also see parts of the township and the mountains in the distance. The BMX track was in need of some improvement here and there, but it was fit for purpose. There was a small group of young boys at the start gate, happy and practising their skills together enthusiastically, testing their jump starts and their riding abilities across the ramps and berms. I turned to Sipho and said, 'Khayelitsha is a real tough place for people, isn't it?'

He pointed to the road by the entrance gate and answered, 'Yes, it can be, and it was. This road here, that highway there, it was regarded as being one of the most dangerous places in the country for all the robberies and murders that had taken place over the years, but it's pretty quiet here today, Dr Marlon.'

'What!?' To me it looked like a normal road, adjacent to what was a sanctuary for the young people of the township.

I returned to Khayelitsha the following morning to meet with teachers and community leaders from across the Western Province that Sipho had helped me recruit for the coaching programme that I had devised. I would be training them in a combination of skills, including bike-handling and racing drills for the disciplines of road, track, mountain-biking and cyclo-cross, and basic mechanical servicing that the teachers and community leaders could use in their future work with young students. We found that some of the teachers themselves couldn't ride a bike, so we had to teach them and by the end of the course they were new riders. Before I left the academy I shared my work on Black cycling champions to an audience of young children, teenagers and adults. We sat outside in the car park during a load-shedding period. This is a regular and widespread national electricity blackout that has been occurring in the country since 2007, supposedly due to insufficient generation capacity. Of course, low-income households and small businesses (occupied more generally by Black people) are the most heavily impacted by this.

One of the teachers on my training course was Amanda Namba. Amanda was representing her women's community cycling development programme, based in Khayelitsha. I'd told Sipho how eager I was to get out for a ride, so Litha lent me his road bike so I could take a ride with Sipho and Amanda across Cape Town.

The next morning, we rode together steadily for around 80 kilometres. This included a climb up to Chapman's Peak on the Atlantic Coast between Hout Bay and Noordhoek. The views across the ocean were stunning. The winding turns, the draggy climbs and the speedy descents all made for a very special bicycle ride. Here was just a little bit of South Africa in all its natural beauty. Then, to my surprise, we approached a seaside village called Llandudno. I couldn't believe it. This is quite a difficult Welsh name to pronounce, but here, as a result of British colonialism, was a distinct piece of Wales in South Africa.

There were so many groups of riders spinning past us in the opposite direction during our ride. I noticed that none, if any, featured Black riders. I asked Sipho whether the Velokhaya riders came out this far to see things. He told me that only the more experienced ones who were more skilled at riding did. I said I hoped more of the younger ones would do so in the future, to see how far the bicycle can take them and to see the natural beauty of their country.

I returned to South Africa six months later to work with Velokhaya Life Cycling Academy in Bethlehem, Free State Province, a town around 1,250 kilometres northeast from Cape Town and around 70 kilometres north of the border with Lesotho. My visit to South Africa was going to be a short trip, but I wanted to meet and converse with Black cyclists, cycling coaches and cycling community leaders in hard-to-reach areas like Bethlehem, to find out what they thought about the representation of Black cyclists at national level in South Africa. I also intended to visit Black cyclists in Johannesburg and Soweto to get their thoughts about this.

When I arrived at Oliver Tambo International Airport in Johannesburg I was instantly drawn to the huge statue of Tambo, who was a significant leader of the anti-Apartheid struggle and president of the African National Congress from 1967 to 1991. Unfortunately, though, I couldn't take time to absorb all this history as I had to rush for my connecting flight to Bloemfontein. I knew that my bags would be delayed. But it was better I take the flight than miss it, and the bags follow on.

Bloemfontein was completely different to Cape Town and felt distinctly rural. I later discovered that it had been part of an independent Boer Republic, colonised by the British, and considered the heartland of old South Africa. I had decided to stay here for the journeys to and from Bethlehem as I was going to be joined by Litha and another former Velokhaya rider, Bahle Dwangu. They were flying in from Cape Town to support my cycling coaching work. Bethlehem is almost halfway between Johannesburg and Bloemfontein, but as they told me they had never been to Bloemfontein, I chose this as our base. I hired a large 4x4 vehicle for the 150-mile, three-hours-each-way drive to Bethlehem. Each day we had to make a very early start, but on both days this was rewarded with a stunning view of the sunrise over the Drakensberg mountain range, which follows the Lesotho border.

On arrival at the community in Bethlehem where we were going to be working, it was clear to see how tough the living conditions were. People were living out of corrugated iron shacks. There was trash being burned in a field close to where some young people were playing football barefoot. But the primary school was in wonderful condition. I was greeted by the Velokhaya leader in Bethlehem, Jacob Lempe, who was also the school's headteacher. We'd be using his school's playground for our coaching activities. Following some of our early morning activities, and during our lunch, I asked what he thought about Black representation in South African cycling at a national level and he said:

'If we look into how cycling has been presented, this has been as a white-dominated sport. Black people are a majority in this country, but when it comes to elite cycling they are in the minority within the majority of white people. It's important to share that Black people do

97

have talent and potential to excel in this sport. This is a message that needs to be communicated across the Black community.'

The cycling coaching programme that I had introduced to Velokhaya was designed as a teacher education intervention for their professional development, and in equipping them with the skills to transform their school grounds into cycling facilities that could enable coaching young people in multiple disciplines such as track racing, mountain biking and cyclo-cross. The aim was to show how cycling as a sport could develop at grassroots community level at low cost, carried out in a safe environment, and be accessible to all as a possible pathway to future national and international representation in the sport. Testing the programme at grassroots level, working alongside teachers, cycling coaches and community leaders, was essential and I encouraged Litha and Bahle to lead the sessions.

Following Bethlehem and Bloemfontein, I returned to Johannesburg with two days left to absorb as much as I could about cycling in South Africa. From Johannesburg, I had organised to travel to Soweto township to meet Mpumelelo Mtintso, a cycling leader, entrepreneur and founder of Book Ibhoni. He opened this as a quiet space in the community where people could come with their bikes to relax and read a book. The word 'ibhoni' means 'bicycle' in Soweto slang and as well as hiring out bikes to local people he was dealing in books for sharing, so he named his store Book Ibhoni. Mpumelelo told me that although he wasn't a racer, he'd travelled around the country and abroad, and seen how people used bicycles, and that's how he became interested in promoting cycling in his community. He now organises 'riding for a purpose' events, like the Tour de Libraries, where people cycle to community libraries to donate books. I loved what Mpumelelo was doing and thought this was such a wonderful way of showing a connection with cycling and educational leadership in the local community.

Book Ibhoni is now a dynamic cycling social enterprise that organises cycling tours for national visitors and international tourists, who want to learn more about the history of Soweto as a significant place of Black leadership during the anti-Apartheid struggles. I asked him for his views on whether things had become better or worse for Black people and Black-led cycling clubs after the end of Apartheid. He said:

'Cycling is still seen as a "white" sport in South Africa, and it's dominated by white people. However, some things are improving in Black communities in terms of cycling. A lot of cycling clubs, like Banditz Bicycle Club, are coming up and doing well. But the access to the sport at a higher level will always be a challenge for Black people due to many factors, like expensive bicycles and gear.'

Like everyone else I'd met in South Africa who had answered this question, the problem is money. Aspirant cyclists in the Black majority are rooted in significant financial disadvantage compared to the white minority. Their financial strength will buy them resources for supporting the development pathway that can secure their future representation in the sport for South Africa at international level. Mpumelelo added, 'We don't have a lot of "Nice Dlaminis" to look up to. Even him, he didn't get far. It's so sad.' I asked him what needs to be done to get more Black riders into road racing, track cycling and mountain biking, and he said: 'The best way would be to introduce the sport to schools. That way, kids can learn and enjoy the sports at a young age. At home it's difficult, because some of these kids have to be adults at home and take care of sick parents.' This conversation gave me lots to think about in coming to a greater sense of knowing about the social and economic circumstances of young Black people in his community.

I was thrilled that Mpumelelo had organised for me to give a talk about my *Black Champions in Cycling* book to the young people of Soweto Cycling Team, who looked resplendent in their green and black cycling kits. I shared with them some stories in the book, introducing them to Major Taylor, Rahsaan Bahati, Maurice Burton, Russell Williams and others. They probably hadn't heard of these riders, but now they had the opportunity to discover and learn, and possibly become inspired too. Still, at the same time I knew that these young riders had their own rich history of Black champion cyclists from the gold mines era whom they probably didn't know about either. I shared all the names and stories I knew, and suggested they carry out further research themselves.

The young riders were being looked after by Buhle Madlala, co-founder of the National Cycling Academy Forum (NCAF), a collective of 32 academies operating as one organisation and representing rural and township Black cycling enthusiasts who felt excluded from mainstream cycling. She explained:

'I co-founded NCAF with cycling activists Bruce Malele of Sampada Cycling and Bonga Nqgobane, who is the only Black Commissaire [cycling official equivalent to referee or umpire] in South Africa. We challenged the authorities and administrators of Cycling South Africa at the 2016 National Indaba [conference]. It had been 22 years since the 1994 democratic elections, yet no grassroots policy and diversity, inclusion and development policy was in place. I wanted an advocacy group that would hold the cycling federation accountable. The provincial administration and the executive are not transformed. There has been a "total blackout" when it comes to training of officials, event organisers, accreditations and the selection of Black cyclists in premium events, as well as Black representation on the world stage.'

Buhle's testimonies echoed loudly with the email message that I had been sent earlier in the year from South Africa concerning systemic racism, on how grassroots cycling clubs from Black townships and rural Black communities feel dismissed, marginalised in terms of training developments and racing opportunities, and ignored for important cycling events that could possibly lead their riders towards national and international racing in the future. I asked her about the relationship between the self-empowered, Black-led NCAF and the dominant white South African national cycling body and she said that transformation remains a pie-in-the-sky idea; that there is no willingness to nurture and profile emerging non-white cyclists who consistently take podiums and are on form. She also spoke of nepotism and result-rigging as being rife at competitions across the country, and she told me how selection criteria is not publicly shared and how only those who can afford to travel can represent South Africa. Buhle was of the view that the lead organisation for cycling in South Africa could not be the organisation to foster change, because it had created the problem to begin with and that is why NCAF exists – to enact genuine transformation in the sport for young Black cyclists.

The powerful drive and leadership for delivering social justice for marginalised Black cycling groups comes through an NCAF 'ubuntu' network in which cycling group members can share knowledge and resources to enable each other to live their best cycling lives, aside from the white-dominated cycling system of inequity.

In my conversation with one of the leaders at the Velokhaya Life Cycling Academy, I was told: 'We've raised these issues on many platforms. There was an independent report that was done after we raised these issues and more. It found that there was racism, lack of transformations and many other things. They [Cycling South Africa] were then told they need to transform.' The independent inquiry and report into the accusations of racism was completed in October 2020 by Ayanda Tsikayi Attorneys Inc. on the instruction of Cycling South Africa President Ciska Du-Plessis Austin. The transformation has been that some of Velokhaya Life Cycling Academy riders, due to their talent and on their own merit, have won their home BMX National Championships and BMX national series events, and have gone on to represent South Africa at the UCI BMX World Championships in France 2022 and Glasgow 2023. I was able to contribute to their development of a network of support and influence for when they came to Europe in preparation for their World Championship events. I linked them up with the Peckham BMX Club, led by expert coaches CK Flash and Nigel Whyte, and one of the leading clubs in the UK. CK is a seminal coach, and Nigel is the father of the British Olympic and World Championships medallists Kye Whyte and Tre Whyte. Connections were made and training sessions were shared, with this becoming a new international community link for both Velokhaya Life Cycling Academy and Peckham BMX.

In terms of Black South African rider representation across the disciplines of road and track cycling, out of the 50,486,856 Black people recorded in the census of 2022 from an overall population of 61,988,314, I'd hope that many more cyclists will emerge in the short and long term, building on the relative successes of Songezo Jim and of Nicholas Dlamini, but only time will tell. One way of accelerating this possibility could be through the use of racial quotas to make the national road and track cycling team demographically more representative. This plan of action for cycling would be supported and opposed in equal measures. Racial quotas were implemented in some South African sports in 2016 to accelerate and increase the representation of Black athletes at international level across the sports of cricket, rugby union and netball. The South African government told the sport's governing body that the rugby union team for the 2019 World Cup in Japan should consist of 50 per cent Black players.

One argument for the application of racial quotas is that positive discrimination is morally correct, because it supports athletes from under-resourced social and economic communities, who don't have the means to showcase their talents, skills and potential on a regular basis in the exclusive spaces where talent-spotting occurs. However, on the other hand some people question whether the cricket, rugby union and netball teams are truly the best of what is available, and believe white people are now facing discrimination in these sports to make room for Black people. Any sporting talent needs to be developed in a stable social and economic environment. In South Africa, white people are more likely to be born into financial advantage and privilege in general than Black people, which gives them a smoother pathway to future sporting excellence. This divide stems from the egregious legacies of racism enacted through European colonialism and the Apartheid system that followed.

Astonishingly to me, some of the criticisms of racial quotas to increase Black representation at national level in South African sport have come from the mouths of leading Black athletes from men's rugby and cricket. Perhaps this is the influence of white ventriloquism, where the Black athlete with a platform becomes a puppet for voicing criticism of a racial quota system. Some Black South African cricket and rugby players have spoken of the 'negative psychological impact' of quota selection, because they felt viewed as 'quota' players, irrespective of their ability. However, this sense of imposter syndrome may also have been produced by their interactions with archaic white mindsets and, for example, some white coaches may not have been able to adapt to working with or being in the presence of Black athletes.

The quota systems are to provide equity in the growth and development of Black athletes in representation and for white athletes and coaches to support this too. Black athletes could argue that the dominant presence of white athletes and coaches are also falsely merited, by the wealth and privileges they gained from their parents and grandparents during colonial rule and Apartheid, and therefore their presence on the national team makes them just as much an imposter.

Any possible future use of racial quotas for Black cycling athletes in representing South Africa in road racing, track cycling, mountain biking, and more, also needs to be same for Black cycling coaches, Black cycling administrators, Black cycling medical staff, if the cycling culture at national level is really going to transform by the enactment of social justice.

From my interpretation of the issue, both supporters and opponents of the racial quota system for national sports representation in South Africa agree that the grassroots development is where genuine and lasting sporting transformation will occur through integrated interventions at multiple levels of society. This is the view that meets with all of the people that I met with and spoke with on visiting Velokhaya. My work was designed to improve access into under-resourced communities in rural areas and townships which are brimming with the talent of so many Black people in South Africa. I hoped that this implementation in schools, teacher education and community development could be one of many triggers for contributing to a revolution of change and opportunity for Black people and cycling in the country.

9

(Dis)graced in the red, white and blue

I was interested in watching some of the 2023 Tour de Lunsar, a bike race held since 2016 in the town of Lunsar, in west-central Sierra Leone, West Africa. I'd followed this race over the years, particularly when it was screened live on Instagram in 2022. I was looking to see its developments. The first day of the 2023 event would be separate races for junior men and women competitors, so I switched between the Lunsar Cycling Team social media platforms to check out what was happening. I saw the large crowds gathered around the dome-like Lunsar Clock

Tower building opposite the start/finish line on the Lunsar Road. The voices of the crowd bubbled beneath the occasional hailing of a man's voice from a megaphone. Some of the spectators were standing on the walls, while some of them had climbed higher, on to the Clock Tower roof, to gain a bird's-eye view of the racing.

The images focused on the competitors for the junior men's race on the start line. When I saw this, I immediately grinned and chuckled a question in shock to myself, 'What-the-fuck!?' I was stunned by the sight of multiple riders at the front of the group wearing HSBC UK-sponsored Great Britain national cycling team skinsuits. It was surreal. With all its symbolic associations with European cycling power – World Championship and Olympic glory of the past and in recent times – the red, white and blue of Great Britain was being worn by a line-up of unknown young African cyclists with their steel-framed bicycles. They looked anxious. They would be unaware of my critical Black-British viewpoint which saw Great Britain's red, white and blue as invading their unique African cycling space, robbing them of their moment. I perceived that somebody in Sierra Leone had instructed this grotesque display in complicity with somebody else from the UK. This to me was cycling poverty prostitution, framing the representation of young African cyclists in connection with the red, white and blue, in a financial sponsorship appeal to white British eyes, minds, wallets and purses.

This new spectacle was even more peculiar than images I'd seen of the previous year's event, which showed some of the riders wearing oversized cycling helmets that were slipping from the sides of their heads in their wild celebrations. Some were draped in branded USA and Australian national cycling team kits. The riders were being held aloft by spectators; their mouths wide open from the strain of their racing efforts, sweat dripping from their faces, fists pumping the sky to the elation of their supporters. This photography was raw and communicated a vivid passion for the sport. Still, I could not avoid being struck by the absurdity of these elated African riders outfitted in cultural and ethnically identifiable symbolic national colours of dominant white peopled nations. The African riders that I saw wore no distinctive cycling clothing in identifying and representing their own cultural and national identities.

For me, the most outrageous photographic image shared across social media of the 2023 Tour de Lunsar was of a shoeless cyclist in the junior race. Here was a young man, racing on an undersized child's 24-inch wheelset bicycle with tapeless steel handlebars. His face was grimaced as he rode on, even more so were the faces of the shocked roadside spectators watching him. He wore white socks, his toes curled over spindles on the cranks that seemed to be without any pedal plates. This was an ugly sight to me. I somehow felt embarrassed for the rider, but some social media accounts on discussing this image seemed to think that at least the rider was graced by his wearing the red, white and blue HSBC UK-sponsored Great Britain national cycling team skinsuit, as a social media post from a British sponsor of the race put it: 'Why are we involved in the Tour de Lunsar? This photo explains why . . . This chap cycling yesterday covered 90k wearing NO SHOES and a @BritishCycling strip . . . When the cycling community comes together it's a brilliant thing.'

To me, this was lazy, uncritical and self-congratulatory, presenting the young African rider in English terms: 'This chap', a rudimentary soul – an unknown to them, their spectacle of the 'other'. In fact, his name is Lamin Bangura. The comments whiffed of paternalistic European pity for the poor and dependent African and brought to mind colonial writer Rudyard Kipling's 1899 poem, 'The White Man's Burden', that puts forward the imperialist proposition that white people are morally obliged to civilise non-white peoples, because they are less developed. Nonetheless, this superficial narrative of altruism created a roar of UK social media cheerleading and virtual pats on the back given to the people who donated the cycling kits. But from what I saw, the con was bought by many. The red, white and blue HSBC UK Great Britain national cycling team skinsuits were past their 'use by date' through a defunct sponsorship deal and therefore unwanted by their owners. These kits were binned in the dumping ground of Africa. Still, maybe this was at least no worse than passing over to the African riders the more immediate Great Britain cycling team kit with its familiar Shell Oil sponsorship logo: a symbolic representation of British colonial and neo-colonial extraction of Africa's rich mineral wealth through the Shell Oil refineries in the Western area of Sierra Leone.

I had seen similar virtue signalling before, when the Ugandan cyclist Charles Kagimu won the African Men's Road Time Trial championship in 2023. Writing on X (formerly Twitter), one cycling journalist highlighted that Kagimu did this on the 2022 time trial bike that had previously belonged to INEOS Grenadier road racer Luke Rowe, and that Kagimu had also attended an INEOS training camp earlier in the year, and been given other equipment by the team, too. For me, what was really being implied was that Kagimu could not possibly advance his athletic capabilities without European resources and investment in him. The central focus it seemed from the journalist was that the INEOS-owned bike and training camp had transformed the African rider to a different state of being. After this, I spoke with Kagimu on Instagram messenger saying: 'That thing on Twitter. I guess what I wanted to take focus away from the original writer was the borrowed use of the bike as being the reason for success, to a respectable focus on the actual athlete. One thing I was told when I was a racer: "It's not the bike, but the rider on it". The bike can help but the rider is the engine.' Charles responded to me with a love heart emoji, saying, 'That's very right'.

In the UK, and for most of the Western world, we've been raised on the persistent discourse of seeing and knowing Africa as the uncivilised and underdeveloped world; Africa as the wastebin for our unwanted and redundant items from our excesses of consumerism: the clothes, the shoes, the bikes and more. The Oxfam and Save the Children charity shops on UK high streets remind us that our items of trash have a place in Africa. If we bring it there and leave it, we can feel good about ourselves, because we are doing good for others, because Africa is in need. That Africa in constant need is so entrenched in our mindset that even some Black-led cycling groups from the UK in their 'brand partnerships' with white-owned cycling businesses have made it their mission to travel annually as envoys to countries in Africa on cycling crusades of so-called 'Black unity'. They bring with them discontinued and unwanted cycling stock from the UK market for the Africans that they meet to pick from.

In fact, I met and spoke with one African cycling charity leader who had experienced this. She wanted to remain anonymous for this book, but she showed me that she had been given around 25 pairs of cycling shoes, but they didn't have the necessary cleats and pedals for immediate use. She had no way to obtain these items, as her charity was based in a rural part of the country, a four-hour drive from the capital city, with no specialist bike shop or the funding to obtain the cleats and pedals for the shoes. The cycling shoes remained unused, gathering dust in the boxes that they came in from the UK.

According to Paul Kagame, president of the central-east African Republic of Rwanda, 'God did not put this great African continent and its people – over 1.3 billion – and decide that they will go to waste just to live in poverty, fed by others, pitied, abused, assisted, and you believe it? How is that possible?' But there has been criticism of this. The educator, author and consultant in Socioeconomic Development & Governance, David Himbara, describes Kagame's 'braggadocio' and discourse as a 'big lie'. This view relates to the fact that Rwanda and other African countries like Sierra Leone, where the Tour de Lunsar takes place, are both classified by the International Monetary Fund as among the 25 'poorest and most vulnerable members' currently receiving debt relief. But, for me, I feel that I see Kagame's intentions with his language. And if this is a lie to be repeated again and again and often enough as a psychological propaganda, as his critics have claimed, well maybe it will be enough of a lie to become known as the truth for believing and for giving hope, motivation, aspiration and self-determination to the under-resourced, poor and oppressed people of the African continent. To become self-dependent and autonomous is the freedom that is desired.

I took my thoughts and concerns to some cyclists from the Sierra Leone cycling scene. I asked them about their wearing cycling clothing kits that were donated from abroad, including the national colours of Great Britain, USA and Australia. Tenesie Dixon, co-founder and captain of the Flames Cycling Team from Sierra Leone's capital city, Freetown, said:

'Most of the guys will buy their kits from the market from whatever comes in from the containers from Europe. Some jerseys are bought along the way, and some are given as donations. But we [Flames Cycling Team] have our own jersey and kits in the Sierra Leonean colours of white, green, black and blue. Our jersey sponsor is Fambul, a Sierra Leonean community empowerment organisation.'

The junior male winner of the race in 2022, Ibrihim Kamara of the C2C cycling team, also from Freetown, said, 'For me, I'm not happy seeing that. I am sure this is being done for maybe money or more sponsorships. It will be great if we started putting on our own kits.' I spoke with the 2016 Sierra Leone national cycling champion, Isata Sama Mondeh, who was pictured winning the Tour de Lunsar in 2021, wearing a distinctive red, white and blue USA cycling skinsuit. Now an executive member of the Sierra Leone Cycling Association, she said, 'Now, every rider is with a club and if they are going for a competition, they must use their club jersey.'

There seems to be a change for the better in the mindsets of some of the teams and riders from Sierra Leone. This could mean that in future line-ups of the Tour de Lunsar the cycling kits on display will be represented by the ethnic and cultural distinctions and imaginations of African cyclists, and won't depend on the unwanted, outdated national cycling kits of the USA, Australia and Great Britain that have been binned in Africa.

10

European illusions in African dreams

There was one Sierra Leonean rider that I was interested in seeing in the 2023 edition of the Tour de Lunsar – Fatima (Deborah) Conteh. She had been developing strongly over the years as a racer and had won the women's race in 2022. This victory had attracted some international attention from the Canyon-SRAM Generation team, who in 2022 had announced their development of an ethnically diverse portfolio of women riders, with many from Global South countries. Deborah had received an invite to join the team in Germany, but she had reached out to me just after her Tour de Lunsar victory to tell me of the struggles that she was facing to take up this opportunity to race outside Sierra Leone and pursue her ambition to race in Europe. Here is part of her letter:

'Dear Dr Marlon,
I just came back from Ghana yesterday after having a lot of stress getting my visa to travel to Spain to join my new cycling club Canyon-SRAM Generation. I was there to race and attend a visa appointment, but all of a sudden I was not allowed, because the Spanish embassy in Ghana only issued visas to Ghanaian residents. I returned back yesterday with a lot of stress, because my manager tells me that he didn't have money again to send me to Ivory Coast, which is the only nearby country where I can get a Spanish Schengen visa. Overall, we have spent over 3,500 US dollars to travel two times in Ghana. My first travel I applied for a German ID work visa and attended the appointment at the German embassy in Accra, but all of a sudden, they refused to give me the visa.'

So much valuable time and so much money all lost and for Deborah a stressful nightmare experience in pursuing her dream to ride in Europe. This nightmare of trying to obtain a visa to enter Europe is not unique to this one rider. When I spoke with other elite and professional African cyclists, they shared accounts of the barriers that they had faced. The Ugandan rider Charles Kagimu told me:

'When I am preparing for a race and I am thinking about the visa situation, it affects my mental capacity. It increases my stress levels. Most countries in my part of Africa do not have embassies. If I can't travel from Nairobi where I am based, I have gone elsewhere to travel. Having to apply for a visa doesn't put you in [a] great situation, depending on the relationship between the country you are from and the country you are applying for. East African countries were colonised by Britain. You expect them to have embassies that have decision-making, but the visa application must go to South Africa instead. The issues I have had with visas are to do with cycling. The process is hard for all African cyclists. I know white cyclists from Africa have had some problems, but not as huge as the Black cyclists. It's more about colour. I think those who have the power to issue visas assume this guy, that if he runs away [seeks to escape from having to return to Africa], if he is white, his character will be different. I know some guys who were cyclists have run away after getting a visa, because of the situation in their countries. Some were caught and ended up in refugee camps, but it's a different story the other way around. Most European riders get visas on arrival in Africa. If I have to go racing in Africa, I have to apply for a visa. For Americans, if they need visas, they get them on arrival. They get visas in a day or two, but for me, it could be weeks.'

Charles Kagimu

Kagimu raced in the Tour du Rwanda in 2022, finishing 21st overall. This was among a field of racers that included an Under-23 Great Britain national team. These riders were able to travel from Europe to Africa for their racing with ease, all covered by a 30-day tourist visa, at no cost. Charles' testimony indicates that nationality, citizenship and, most significantly, the skin colour of the rider are key visa permission determinants. This was confirmed when I discussed this issue with Kenyan champion cyclist Sule Kangangi, who regrettably is now deceased after a fatal bike crash during a gravel endurance race in 2022:

'I have missed a few races because of visas. The issue . . . of people going to Europe and running away means we are being tarred by the same brush. Is this racism? I think it's racism. The goal posts are set differently for different people. I don't think if it were a white person from Kenya, he would be treated the same.'

When I spoke about the issue with the Rwandan cyclist Adrien Niyonshuti, who at the time was in a leading coaching role with racing cyclists in Benin, he said:

'I have one rider since January to May, he cannot get a visa. I applied on time for the visa. Two times I did Olympics with visa. I applied for visa to go to Britain, in 2017. I was not able to get visa. I ended up losing my contract. I remember Daniel Teklehaimanot [of Eritrea] had lots of issues to stay in Australia and Europe. We still have a lot of problems with visas. The Black cyclist is having a tough time to stay in Europe.'

However, how does the idea of racing in Europe form in the minds of Black people from Africa? When I was working in Cape Town, South Africa, Sipho Mona, manager of the Velokhaya Life Cycling Academy, told me some of his story:

'As a rider I always dreamt of riding in the Tour de France and in Europe. It became an obsession after having watched the Tour and the Giro, which were the only events televised back in the 90s by the media. In hindsight it was a dream planted in my mind by the media, as it was the only thing I was fed besides my reality of racing in and around South Africa, which I loved as well. It was also a bit of a farfetched dream as there were no Black riders in those particular pelotons to aspire to, apart from my teammates in our local racing club.'

When I travelled to Johannesburg to carry out my work with the Velokhaya Cycling Academy I met the experienced former professional

South African road racer Luthando Kaka. He also gave me the sense that Europe is planted in the mind as the only destination for all things of possible greatness in professional cycling for the aspirant Black racing cyclist from Africa:

> 'I could say, through mainstream media and cycling leaders in South Africa, the idea of Europe was planted in my head. As a rider coming from Khayelitsha, Cape Town, my early cycling dreams were to race against and measure my abilities outside of Khayelitsha, then Cape Town, South Africa, Africa and the rest of the world, and in that specific order. Being told and understanding early on that cycling was bigger in Europe, more professional and more rewarding, I wanted to have that experience and get a shot at success on a world stage.'

I spoke with Jean Pierre Rumashana, co-founder of Team Unity Cycling of Rwanda, and he told me, 'Africa's best riders want to race in Europe, because it is where they will get enough races. It is where they see competitions.' His fellow Rwandan Adrien Niyonshuti shared with me his early development as a racing cyclist in Rwanda. He gave me some insights into the external support and influence from white people that he received, with Europe being the ultimate destination for becoming a professional cyclist planted firmly in his mind:

> 'Jock Boyer opened my mind to being a professional cyclist. Jock was the first American to race in the Tour de France . . . It was nice for him to come to Rwanda. Cycling is a big factory. You need to know people who can get you the shoes, dress, support with visa. Outside of South Africa there is no other country that can help you to get the connections, equipment, shoes, jerseys. Europe is 120 years in front of Africa. If you want to be a good cyclist, you must move to Europe. Africa cannot organise races for 150 racers. The peloton must improve if they want to create a platform for African riders.'

It is interesting to contrast this view of Europe where all that glitters is gold against the views given to me from the leader of a cycling team from Eritrea called the May Stars. When I contacted them, I spoke with Aklilu Haile, a racer and co-founder of the team. He told me that May Stars are a fusion of Rwandan and Eritrean professional cyclists. I wanted his perspectives about the power of European influences on the development of cycling in Africa, particularly in the Eastern area of the continent something that he said May Stars are aiming to resist:

'Definitely there are many influences trying to make the African dependent. But if we stand in our mission, we can overcome and be competitors, not dependent. May Stars is an idea initiated for more than 12 years. As current sports director, and as a former rider, I was never happy seeing African riders, and especially Eritrean riders, exploited. I reject it when young talented Eritrean riders go to UCI centres [in Europe and Africa] and are later called out [credited] as a product of the UCI centre. With this in mind I initiated this idea of starting a continental [mixed African] team, May Stars, to give opportunity to Eritrean riders and African riders to be competitive and guide them to develop their knowledge and protect themselves from exploitation. From my experiences in Eritrea, all riders who joined UCI centres were our best riders and the UCI take the credit for doing nothing.'

Haile feels strongly that the best Eritrean riders are born, grown and developed early on by their country, and this bond is being compromised, particularly via the magnetic pull of the European finishing school of the UCI World Cycling Centre in Aigle, Switzerland, and its African satellite in the city Paarl, South Africa, which opened in 2005. Some of the finished articles from Eritrea include the likes of Daniel Teklehaimanot and Merhawi Kudus, while Biniam Girmay and Henok Mulubrhan have both trained at Aigle in Switzerland. All have gone on to perform with professional cycling teams well away from Eritrea and generally in Europe. On the surface of things, this may look like a considerate approach by the UCI in offering schooling and development of Africa's best up-and-coming talent.

Still, I do understand Aklilu Haile's sense of European exploitation of the best up-and-coming African cyclists as a continuation of colonial extraction of riches from the African continent. This European motivation has its origins in the formal partitioning of African territories by European nations following the 1884–85 Berlin Conference. This conference was organised by Otto von Bismarck, the first chancellor of Germany, at the request of Leopold II of Belgium. The European nations claimed that by colonising Africa they were also exporting civilisation to a continent which they regarded as backward and undeveloped. In fact, this 'Scramble for Africa' and its riches by European countries and nations had been occurring way before the 1884–85 Berlin Conference, and this has included the continuous robbery of African knowledge in arts, culture, science and music, and the theft of gold, diamonds, oil, rubber, coffee, tea, land and of African people themselves through European enslavement and the transatlantic slave trade. So much more has been extracted from the African continent though theft and exploitation, but this new wave of extracting cycling riches from Africa has been argued as beneficial for African people for their development and advancement in the sport.

Jean-Pierre Van Zyl, head of the UCI World Cycling Centre's South African satellite in Paarl, has commented, 'Africa is a gold mine of talent. The most talent in the entire world sits within Africa. It's a question of extracting it' – and the exploitative European colonial rhetoric of 'gold mine' and 'extracting' from Africa is direct and evident. The justification given is to teach the African continent's national federations to become autonomous, to foster partnerships, to provide education and equipment, to provide support and guidance with organising events, and to provide opportunities to apply for development money through UCI solidarity funding, their programme created in 2018. All of this may sound very reasonable, but in my view, it presents as a paternalistic European influence and control of Africa's cycling destiny, re-enacting the 19th-century colonial power-dynamic as a contemporary neo-colonial lock. By the central design of a Eurocentric framework of authority and influence located on the African continent that is the UCI World Cycling Centre in Paarl, South Africa, African national cycling federations engaging in this relationship take the position of subordination to a 'superior' European knowledge and pathway as the singular route to their full sense of development and achievement under European judgement. By these exchanges and debts of tutorage, African cycling will always be dependent on the central European power, the UCI. They hold the cards.

There is no genuine African autonomy in innovation and vision for cycling where there is paternalistic European influence and colonisation in the leadership of African cyclists and their cycling clubs and federations. And there are many relationships of this kind across the continent in European cycling's own 'Scramble for Africa'. Any outstanding young African cyclist identified by solidarity funding, the athlete development programme, as having the potential to become a rider for the UCI World Tour becomes like the prized ivory of the Black rhinoceros, a trophy item for the showcase of white-led teams based in both Europe and Africa.

From the mid-2000s, African-based, white-led teams like Team Quebheka were the first to engage in Black cyclist trophy-hunting. They could draw riches from their established colonial base in South Africa to carry out their Black cyclist headhunting exploits. With the support of the World Cycling Centre, in Paarl, South Africa, they managed to bring in the likes of Eritreans Daniel Teklehaimanot and Merhawi Kudus, and later, of course, Nicholas Dlamini. The German professional cycling team Bike Aid had also been headhunting for Black cyclist talent since 2007 around the Eastern African area. They brought in the likes of Sule Kangangi and Salim Kipkemboi from Kenya; Dawit Yemane, Henok Mulubrhan and Mekseb Debesay from Eritrea; and Eric Muhoza of Rwanda. But, curiously again, like Team Quebheka, as a professional cycling team Bike Aid has consisted of a majority of white riders from Europe.

The accusation of tokenism can easily be directed at white rider-dominated teams appearing on the racing scene in Africa and Europe when it seems that, by the solitary representation of a Black rider face among them, they are marketing their cycling brand. On this, the South African rider Luthando Kaka told me, 'Teams have been using Black riders for their poverty and hardship stories rather than athletic capabilities and achievements. I also found it disturbing that there would be one Black rider at a time in a team, because they can do one Black poverty story at a time.' This narrative conceals the ambitions and interests of the white rider-led cycling teams. Kaka added, 'White riders get the preferential treatment when it comes to longevity in the sport. Black people at the top of the sport are there for a very short time, maybe three to four years, and they are gone while their white counterparts stay for much longer in the sport.'

Despite Kaka's stark observations, he acknowledged a developing sense of equitable action by some World Tour cycling teams, particularly for Black riders from Africa with the Trek-Segafredo cycling team. They had four Eritreans out of six Black riders from Africa in their 2023 UCI World Tour Team, and he commented, 'I'm happy there's a change, by Trek-Segafredo. Also, another positive has been the well-planned development of riders in Eritrea and Rwanda, which we are starting to see, as in the past there was a feeling that riders are shipped into the Europe scene, milked dry and shipped back to Africa.' Kaka's comments about riders being shipped to and from Europe and back to Africa after being 'milked dry' echoes the concerns voiced earlier by Aklilu Haile. That African dream of a move to Europe for racing is counterbalanced by the experiences of Fatima Deborah Conteh and even Luthando Kaka himself, who told me, 'I lacked a clear path in cycling, having reached Europe as I felt homesick. I spent three months at the UCI school of cycling in Aigle [Switzerland], when I was asked to extend my stay for a year, but I chose to go back home to South Africa to further my university studies in 2004.' The implication given is that Kaka left Europe before he was 'milked dry'.

From some of the testimonies in this chapter it seems that the influence of the European Tour de France and Giro d'Italia narrative has spread like a holy Christian gospel across Africa, convincing aspirant Black racing cyclists that to get to heaven to 'become', they must leave Africa behind; they must dream of Europe and take action to move to Europe. It is as though history is repeating itself through cycling; just as the original European Christian missionaries set up churches across Africa to convince Africans to convert to Christianity, European-led cycling development sites are being built in African locations as centres for similar forms of indoctrination. In June 2022, the INEOS Group, owners of the INEOS Grenadiers UCI World Tour cycling team, announced the opening of their cycling academy in Iten, Kenya. At the time, Sir David Brailsford, general manager of INEOS Grenadiers, said, 'This is a significant and exciting development in world cycling – it has the power to drive lasting change by developing new riders from Africa.'

To me, by setting out to develop and advance the 'rudimental' African through a 'New Testament' of cycling, INEOS is assuming 'the white man's burden' and Brailsford's announcement chimes with the words of Jean-Pierre Van Zyl that I shared earlier. INEOS' presence in Africa can be seen as a British colonial gold-digging venture, with anything precious that emerges from its investment on African ground belonging to them. From this, they will be able to teach their African prodigies the European narrative and the Grand Tour-winning gospels of Wiggins, Froome, Geraint Thomas and more, leading Black people of Africa to their way, their truth and their word, on the dream of a pathway to a cycling heaven. For the chosen few perhaps they will see no more European illusions in their African dreams.

11

'They'll be crowning white kings and white queens of world cycling – in Africa!'

In September 2021 it was announced that Kigali, capital of Rwanda, would host the 2025 UCI Road World Championships. UCI president David Lappartient said, 'Rwanda ticks all the boxes – organisational, financial and, of course, on a sporting level. We know the passion the fans will bring in Kigali. There will be a million fans out for the event. It will be amazing . . .'

In this example of the European giving and African receiving 'interest-convergence' with Rwanda being named the 'first ever' African country to host the event, I was curious to see cycling fans and media reactions to this news. An interesting exchange that was made for public viewing on social media caught my attention. One UK cycling news commentator spoke of shock and concern at the decision made by the UCI. He shared quotations from a 2020 Amnesty International report which implicated the current regime in Rwanda as responsible for 'enforced disappearances', 'arbitrary detention', 'excessive use of force', 'unfair trials' and 'restrictions on the right to freedom of expression'. In the discussion that followed, one respondent argued that by taking this view of Rwanda, then perhaps other global sporting events should not have and could not ever occur in countries such Qatar, Germany, South Africa, Chile, China, Argentina, Russia and more, due to past and current repressive regimes. Another respondent agreed with this view, arguing that if South Africa is included, then all the colonial powers should be cancelled in the future, with UK, France and Belgium at the top of the list. Arguably the most damning human rights violations of the last 600 years has been the European exploitation of Africa and African people through torture, murder and rape, Apartheid, family displacement, land theft, enforced poverty and systemic racism, inside and outside of the continent. Australia is another nation with this history. European settlement in the 18th century led to massacres and extermination campaigns against indigenous Australians (Aboriginal) between 1788 and 1970. These barbaric actions against humanity did not prevent Australia hosting the 1956 Olympic Games in Melbourne. The thread discussion saw the cycling commentator speaking back, using the original point made about the current regime in Rwanda. But, the validity of this argument was challenged. One of the respondents produced a list of nations viewed currently by the West as being repressive nation states, and yet still able to attract partnership and participation from the West in their hosting of global sport events, for example Qatar (hosts of the 2022 FIFA World Cup) and Formula 1 motorsport events held annually in Saudi Arabia and Bahrain. The thread discussion came to an end with the respondents speaking of looking forward to watching the 2025 UCI Road World Championships in Rwanda.

———

My first view of Rwanda was imposed on me by the images given through BBC television footage reporting on the tragic genocide of 1994 across the country. I simply could not comprehend what I was seeing. I saw mass groups of people chasing their fellow Rwandans with machetes. It was a sight that was too frightening to be real. Experts evaluating population loss in Rwanda have estimated that 800,000 Rwandans died between April and July 1994. For some observers in Europe, perhaps images of the Rwandan genocide confirmed the colonial narratives that were taught in school about the savage behaviours of Black people in Africa. But the Rwandan genocide of 1994 was a deep human tragedy, like the human tragedy of the massacre of 100,000 people and the 'ethnic cleansing' that was occurring at the same time in Europe in the Bosnian War.

However, Africa has always been portrayed as chaotic, dark, ugly and frightening; 'the other world'; the antithesis of Europe and therefore of civilisation. Before the 1994 Rwandan genocide, in the mid-1980s the television news showed me Africa and Black people through the famine in Ethiopia: thousands of Black people, broken, dispirited, motionless in their living-dead, hell-on-Earth existence; skin-and-bone mothers dressed in rags, holding their skin-and-bone crying babies, flies on their bodies, on their heads, in their eyes. In many cases, Africa and Black people continue to be presented by Europe in this way. Some ignorant white people that I have had to teach have thought and spoken about Africa as one country.

Considering what Rwanda had been through in the 1994 genocide and considering this nation's desire to recreate and represent itself as transformed, I initially saw the news of Kigali hosting the 2025 UCI Road World Championships as an outstanding announcement for cycling, for cycling fans, for the nations of Africa and for all African people, but there was a stone in my shoe as well, an uncomfortable feeling that caused the thought in my mind about the event: 'But they'll be crowning white kings and white queens of world cycling – in Africa! – in front of African people!' Images from European colonialism and imperialism that I had absorbed over the years flashed through me. I saw Queen Elizabeth II being carried in a palanquin by a group of bare-chested and barefooted Black porters during a procession to the adulation of a Black audience. I saw the white American Hollywood actor Johnny Weissmuller, swinging freely through the trees in the jungles of Africa as Tarzan, son of an English lord and lady and now king of the apes, able to understand and speak ape language better than Black people who had actually been born and raised in that African space. The white man from outside of Africa, the centre of our attention, jumping down from his jungle ropes to greet his pet chimpanzee – 'Cheeta' – and kissing and hugging his white American girlfriend Jane amidst the background scene of silent Black film extras. I saw Mr Kurtz, the ivory trader and central figure in Joseph Conrad's racist novel *Heart of Darkness*, on his mission through the Congo, I heard his dying words: 'The horror! The horror!'

The 'horror' that I saw was the gross disparities of power, finance and resources between African cycling nations and European cycling nations. Yes, the thought of Black people, African bike racers, being pleased to be able to take part in such a huge cycling event at home, on the African continent, was positive, but to me it was at the cost of being made to look inferior in the races by the overpowering and more experienced competitive European nations and their professional riders. The so-called celebration of world cycling in Africa, in Rwanda, in Kigali, would also cause huge embarrassment due to the racing performances of African cyclists at home, in front of their own people.

Taking pride in the sporting achievements of one's national or continental athletes on home soil is important. I remember it well when Great Britain and the nation revelled in all its gold medallists in the London Olympic Games of 2012. In football, English fans continue to reminisce about the home World Cup win against Germany in 1966 at London's Wembley Stadium. So, was I right to be worried about Black people being embarrassed in the races at the 2025 UCI Road World Championships in Kigali? I reached out directly to some Rwandan cyclists, including those who have lived through decades of development processes in cycling and racing in the country since the genocide of 1994. Jean Pierre Rumashana, the founder of Team Unity Cycling, based in Gitarama, said to me:

'Rwanda, like other countries, has already invested in what they call their best-talented kids. They want to attend and get medals. They do not want to attend for DNFs [Did Not Finishes]. But it will not be easy. You do not prepare a cyclist to take on world champs in just three or five years only. It takes many years to train someone at World Tour level and [many] resources. In terms of organising, I believe it will go as planned [and be] very well organised.'

The pride and desire for success is clear from Jean Pierre. This is not just about African riders making up the numbers in the racing. Rwandans want to see their people among the cyclists being crowned as the kings and queens of world cycling at home in Kigali. But this will be a tough task. Even to qualify to ride in the event will be tough. I spoke with the Ugandan road racer Charles Kagimu, and he agreed:

'I would say the Europeans will be dominant. The world races are extremely long and hard. The qualification system is tough. Europeans are five or six nations and all eligible to bring eight riders. I doubt there will be an African team with more than four or five riders, strong riders. The Belgian team will have top riders in the world rankings. The world champs need a team. If your country is bringing less riders, you have no chance. I hope most African riders qualify.'

The gist of what Kagimu says is mostly accurate and more than likely to happen, particularly when looking at the qualification system for the 2024 UCI Road World Championships for elite men which states:

'Qualification through the UCI World Ranking by nations on 20 August 2024 (200 riders to start)
A. Nations ranked 1 to 10 may enter 8 riders to start (80 riders to start)
B. Nations ranked 11 to 20 may enter 6 riders to start (60 riders to start)
C. Nations ranked 21 to 30 may enter 4 riders to start (40 riders to start)
D. Nations ranked 31 to 50 may enter 1 rider to start (20 riders to start).'

The Nations ranked 1 to 10 at the time of writing were (in order): Belgium, France, Spain, Netherlands, Great Britain, Italy, Denmark,

Australia, Slovenia and the USA. All nations ranked from 11 to 20 were dominant white peopled nations, apart from Colombia (13), Ecuador (18) and Eritrea (20) – the top-listed African nation. The next listed African nation was South Africa (27). Other African nations ranked between 31 and 50 included Algeria (35), Morocco (40), Mauritius (44) and Ethiopia (45). The host nation Rwanda were 62nd in the rankings, and Kagimu's country Uganda were 68th. This means that they cannot qualify riders by national ranking. However, the qualification systems states:

> 'Nations with a rider ranked 1 to 200 in the UCI Individual World Ranking on 20 August 2024 and not yet qualified after provision 1 (A,B,C,D above) may enter 1 rider to start.'

At the time of writing this book Charles' world ranking was 426, and at 726 was the highest ranked Rwandan rider – Moise Mugisha. The UCI Management Committee decides the qualification system each year, but if the current system is kept in place for 2025, a special dispensation will be given to Rwanda as the host nation: 'unless the nation of the country in which the UCI Road World Championships are organised has qualified a minimum of 6 riders to start . . . the concerned nation may enter 6 riders to start.' The Rwandan and Eritrean teams are likely to be the largest African men's teams in Kigali 2025. There is also the possibility that reallocation of entry places will be applied in the case that less than 200 quota places have been allocated. These could go to some African riders in order for them to represent their nations. This may seem to be an equitable action, but in my view, this is only to give a sense of balance in viewing appearances of ethnic representation – those riders/nations offered reallocated places will simply be making up the numbers.

Kagimu has proven himself numerous times on the international stage in races across Africa and has had some decent results in Europe, but he is without a solid national Ugandan team of riders who can perform at the same level as him and support him. If Charles does qualify to race in 2025, he is set to be a one-man-army rider, but no matter how strong you are, it is hard, although not impossible, to win a World Championship road race on your own.

I shared my thoughts and perceptions about representation on the podium at Kigali 2025 during a *Eurosport* interview on 30 March 2022, and I spoke my mind directly:

'. . . they'll be crowning white kings and white queens of world cycling – in Africa, in front of African people'.

On 31 May 2022 a press release from the UCI announced a memorandum of understanding to ensure that African countries are 'well represented with strong podium chances at the UCI's flagship event being held for the first time on the African continent in 2025.' The strategy is to invite cyclists from African countries to a training camp at the UCI World Cycling Centre satellite in Paarl, South Africa. Selected athletes will then be able to train at the UCI World Cycling Centre in Switzerland or elsewhere in Europe, 'where they will gain appropriate race experience over the next three years, in the lead-up to the 2025 UCI Road World Championships in the Rwandan capital and beyond, so they can be competitive by 2025, notably in the Junior and Under 23 categories.'

This intervention by the UCI comes across not as offering equity, but more as providing advance compensation to the Black riders from Africa for the possibility that they will be embarrassed in the World Championship races by their European cyclist guests. The UCI MOU states that this is for African junior and Under-23 riders to 'gain appropriate race experience over the next three years.' But what may be meant by 'appropriate' through what seems a paternalistic gesture? For me, 'appropriate' preparation for an inaugural UCI Road World Championships in Africa means those African riders under the support of the world governing body being not just able to train, but able to compete regularly across Europe, and particularly in the longer races, including the European Classics, and against the riders who are likely to be their main rivals in Kigali 2025. The junior and Under-23 African riders need regular and honest simulations of what to expect among their European competition in preparation for Kigali 2025, and there are junior and Under-23 versions of some of the European Classic races. Regular race conditioning in these such events are vital, otherwise podium after podium in Kigali 2025 is more than likely to be dominated by white riders, decorated with UCI medals and jerseys, flowers and Tissot watches, standing high above the cheering Black spectators. At least in the UCI MOU statement, there is some honesty by their silence on any African rider of note to perform in the senior or elite races. Not seemingly worth any mention, the perception given from this silence on those African riders who seek to qualify for the senior or elite races is, if they do qualify, then they are most unlikely to finish the race, let alone medal.

Sule Kangangi

When I spoke with the Kenyan champion cyclist Sule Kangangi before his death in 2022, I asked him about development opportunities for growing talented cyclists and whether, after Kigali 2025, legacy events should be continued, such as an annual World Tour Classic race. He agreed with my initial thoughts:

'It will be a European "World Championships". It is very likely that the Europeans will win. What can we do to have strong riders by 2025? . . . We need clear structures throughout the year. People are looking for the shortcut for the build-up to 2025. There is really no World Tour Classic. Yes, there is the Tour of Rwanda or Tour of Gabon. Until we have our own races to rival the European races, the difference will continue.'

I also spoke with Adrien Niyonshuti from Rwanda, and he took a different view of the opportunity for cycling in Kigali 2025:

'Celebrate the first country in Africa to host the world champs. This should help with history in developing Africa. It's going to be an opportunity for neighbouring countries to see how the world champs are organised. It will help other neighbouring countries to think they can hold the world champs. If Rwanda are amazing, if after one year or two years or three years, this could leave a legacy. It's promoting cycling in Africa at a high level. I would like to see other countries showing they can organise the African championships. After the world championships, yes, perhaps there could be a Classic race to continue to give the big exposure.'

As part of the World Tour, a world Classic that attracts the best riders from across the globe could become a legacy event to be sustained after 2025. Something similar happened after the 2012 London Olympic Games with the RideLondon events, the first of which, in 2013, was an elite men's race that followed the original London 2012 road race route out to Surrey and was preceded by cycling festivities for the general public. This legacy has been sustained to some extent, although the professional road races for men no longer take place.

I reflected on what Adrien was saying about the need to 'celebrate'. I saw in my mind the unique atmosphere for 2025 that would be created by thousands and thousands of Black people lining the streets to watch the races, and how their presence and their voices would make the event one of greatest celebrations of cycling ever seen. I had watched social media footage of the Tour du Rwanda cycling race over the years, but this race has never been shown on UK television. I felt that I had to get over to Kigali, to witness the event and experience the atmosphere for myself, and to test my perceptions by meeting and talking to people involved with cycling there.

I travelled to Kigali to meet some of the executive members of the Rwandan Cycling Federation (FERWACY). I had been talking to them about the possibility of developing my cycling teacher education project, so I was invited over to discuss my ideas and see the final stage of the 2023 Tour du Rwanda, a 75-kilometre loop around Kigali, starting and finishing at Canal Olympia. This seemed a short distance for a professional road race, but Rwanda is known as the 'land of a thousand hills', so this final stage would indeed be a tough test for the riders.

Arriving in Kigali in the early morning, I was impressed by the ease of travel from the airport to the hotel. There was a lot of traffic, but it all moved smoothly once we got going. There were hills everywhere, with houses and other buildings built at height. I was staying at the Hôtel des Mille Collines, which is depicted in the 2004 Hollywood film *Hotel Rwanda* as a place of refuge for 1268 Rwandans, both Tutsis and Hutus, who were saved from genocide by the hotel's manager, Paul Rusesabagina. There was controversy about the heroic depiction of Rusesabagina, but during my stay I really didn't think too much about the events of 1994, because I was enthralled by the hotel's beautiful Afrocentric art and engrossed in talking to the Rwandans that I met.

FERWACY is made up of executive board members who are either founders or leaders of Rwanda's premier cycling teams. One of these teams, the Benediction Cycling Club, was co-founded in 2005 by Benoit Munyankindi, who at the time of my visit was also General Secretary of FERWACY. Benoit had arranged to collect me and Cordiano Dagnoni, president of the Italian Cycling Federation, and take us to the race. I met Benoit in front of the hotel and got into the car, but Benoit and Cordiano were deep in conversation and there was a long delay before Cordiano went back into the hotel. I wound down the window.

'What is going on, Benoit? Is everything OK? What's the delay?'

'Oh, Dr Marlon, there has been a lot of moving and changing things around. The President, Paul Kagame, will be attending the final stage today. It is a last-minute thing, and we have been up all night, rearranging things.'

'What?! Really?' I said. 'Oh, that's so great that he will attend to support.'

'Yes. This is very big for us, as he has not attended in a while.'

Cordiano returned, having changed out of his blue Team Italia cycling squad tracksuit into more formal clothes, and we set off. On the journey, I spoke to Benoit about cycling in Rwanda and he gave me some of his story:

'I like sport. When I was in secondary school, I tried different sports, but I didn't like contact sports. So I played volleyball and basketball, but with no success. From there, I shifted to running, where I did long distances of 5000 kilometres and 10,000 kilometres. At this time cycling was not developed. In the Western Province of Rwanda, in the Rubavu District, cycling was not among our sports. However, after the 1994 genocide there was a lot of developments in the country through sport. I got the opportunity of being a masseur in the national football team. A young boy among our neighbours was a bicycle taxi. After a short competition of single-speed bike taxis, he came to me requesting extra support so that he would be able to compete at the national level. So, I said, "Yes".

'As for Benediction Cycling Club, I started without knowing of the big important project it will be! In my region, we had never had a cycling team and no rider in the past and cycling was in our mind as a story. This was in 2001 when I helped my boy to go for a one-day race in Kigali. My boy finished 15th out of 32 starting the race. It was from there that I confirmed that Benediction can be possible. I started with one rider and then took on the second rider. When I reached four riders, it was amazing. I made the team. The name I gave was Benediction, which means a prayer asking for divine blessing. I created the Benediction Cycling Team to help young boys and women who haven't anyone to help them, and are from a poor family, but with a talent in cycling to achieve their dreams.'

Benoit successfully led Benediction riders to victory in the African Cycling Championships and to becoming the seminal UCI Continental Team in East Africa.

We arrived at Canal Olympia and queued for COVID tests – they were compulsory because President Kagame was attending the race. We received the all clear and made it to the team presentation ceremony, where we met with more FERWACY executive members who were congregated by the start line. I was introduced to the second vice president, Liliane Kayirebwa, who has been influential in leading the development of cycling across Rwanda for women. I was interested to know more about her role. She told me:

'Rwanda support sports, especially cycling. In our district, Bugesera, cycling is our culture. This is why the leadership of Bugesera decided to found the Bugesera Women's Cycling Team. In 2018 I was a youth leader in my district. So, through elections, I became president of Bugesera Women's Cycling Team and took my position from there with FERWACY. I am the president and legal representative of the Bugesera Women's Cycling Team. The aim is to empower talented girls through riding to unleash their bright future. We also aim at becoming the leading women's cycling team in Rwanda and custodians for sustainable cultural, moral and social-economic development.'

Liliane invited us to take our seats in the pavilion and the riders began to line up. They included a Great Britain Under-23 cycling team and the multiple Grand Tour winner Chris Froome standing together with only two of his teammates remaining in the race from his Israel–Premier Tech team. Also at the start line was the former Tour du Rwanda winner Daniel Teklehaimanot representing Eritrea and another rising star of Eritrea, Henok Mulubrhan, the leader of the race, who was wearing the yellow jersey and representing his team Green Project–Bardiani–CSF–Faizanè of Italy. The event hosts were announced, and the race began to the throbbing synchronised beats of multiple ingoma drummers who were located next to the winner's podium. Following the riders' departure, the large screen showed their movements on the course and the DJ blasted music from the PA system in between race commentary.

In the pavilion I was introduced by Liliane to Pascal Ndizeye Nkunduwite, the owner of Java–InovoTec, a newly formed elite Rwandan cycling team. Pascal had attracted leading Rwandan riders such as Joseph Areruya and Jean Eric Habimana from the disbanded UCI continental ProTouch team. I asked him how he became involved with the Rwandan cycling scene and the goals for his team in the future. He said:

'Once, in 2020, someone invited me to watch the Rwanda National Cycling Championships. Then I became attracted to cycling . . .

Finally, I joined a cycling club from my village as an ordinary member and supporting them financially. A few months later I became the vice president of the cycling club. In 2022, I decided to open a sport company I named Inovotech Ltd. Inovotech is two words – innovation and technology. Cycling shouldn't be left behind to use technology. Inovotech's key point is to empower underprivileged riders and take them to world stages, to give community education about the health benefits of cycling, taking the cycling game to the people.'

There was a pattern in what I was hearing from the Rwandans I was talking to: cycling in their country was very much more than just bike racing. Cycling was being used for community empowerment, health empowerment and educational empowerment for young people, and this was being championed through leaders like Benoit, Pascal and Liliane. Cycling was seen as fuel for national community power, for giving strength to the core of Rwandan society.

Shortly after speaking with Pascal, I was approached by Assia Ingabire and Irenee Bayisabe, both of FERWACY. They invited me to come with them to see if we could follow some of the race in an official Tour du Rwanda car. The race had started some 10 minutes or so earlier, so we would be doing well if we caught up. Sensing this time gap, Bayisabe put his foot down and rallied around the closed roads of the hilly route, which were lined by thousands of spectators. I hung on for dear life in the back of the car, while Ingabire sat coolly in the front passenger seat, texting away on her phone. Bayisabe threw the car about as it screeched around the tight corners. We sped up on the cobblestoned Wall of Kigali, we climbed Rebero Hill, but we still couldn't reach the rear of the race. In the end, we bailed out and returned to the Canal Olympia race finish village. 'Well, thank you very much for that!' I exclaimed as I climbed out of the car. At least I had had a full view of the route, what the riders were going through and the amazing crowds who were there to greet them.

I walked back to the race pavilion with Ingabire and Bayisabe, and we could see that excitement was building. Music was blasting, and the number of spectators inside and outside the village was growing. Then, loud cheers and whistles began to increase in volume as did the synchronised throbbing beats of the ingoma drummers, and mobile phones were held aloft as one of the event announcers proclaimed, 'Ladies and gentlemen! Ladies and gentlemen! Please stand up and welcome his excellency the President of the Republic of Rwanda – Paul Kagame!'

The president, a tall and lean figure of a man, was informally dressed. Relaxed and smiling, he waved at the adoring spectators. Accompanied by the minister of sport for Rwanda, the former professional basketball player, Aurore Mimosa Munyangaju, and surrounded by a number of bodyguards, all dressed from head to toe in black, I watched as Kagame strolled coolly towards the race pavilion. On seeing this, I thought to myself, 'I better get in there quickly to take my seat.' I moved on, swiftly.

I sat watching the race on the big screen, while at the same time watching the president in conversation with the minister of sport, while at the same time watching the president's bodyguards, watching everyone else, but very coolly in a way so as not to make this so apparent. With around five kilometres to go, we were invited by the race management to leave our seats and to stand by the finish line to welcome home the breakaway riders. The president's bodyguards jumped up as he led the way. I followed the large group of pavilion members and we all congregated by the finish line, watching the big screen as the race unfolded to its climax.

The favourite for the stage win was the Eritrean rider, Henok Mulubrhan. He had won stage 3 earlier on in the week, on the back of good form, as he'd won the African Continental Road Race Championships a few weeks earlier in Ghana. I reached into my pocket for my mobile phone, ready to film the final sprint finish. As the race entered the final kilometres, the excitement and anticipation seemed to shift, and the chanting and cheering on the other side of the VIP pavilion changed to soft murmurs and near silence by the finish line, for no reason other than for what they were about to witness in the climax of the race. However, I was standing just in front of an Eritrean fan, and he confirmed that he was by the way he became greatly animated and excited in what he was seeing on the big screen – the prospect of another huge victory for his countryman, Mulubrhan.

The race wound up with around 500 metres to go. At this, the excitement and voices of the spectators grew. Mobile phones were raised above heads to capture the moment of victory for the winner crossing the line. The

Eritrean fan began jumping up and down right by me, his phone in one hand and the other fist pumping the sky while crying out emotionally, 'Go, Henok! Go, Henok! Go, Henok!' At the same time, I felt a punch on my arm and my own mobile phone, which I had been holding aloft, was out of my hand and on the ground. I was down in a flash, frantically searching for it, but I found it, and it wasn't damaged. That was a relief, but as I got up to take the snap, it was too late: the leading riders had flashed across the line, with Mulubrhan arms aloft, taking the victory.

Henok Mulubrhan

'What do you think you're doing?' I called out to the Eritrean fan, but he apologised with a huge smile on his face.

Moments after this we all turned and followed President Kagame and his bodyguards to our seats for the presentation ceremony. The event announcer duo worked well with each other as they spoke in synchrony when calling the names of the race winners to the podium. All of this was accompanied by throbbing synchronised beats of the ingoma drummers. Mulubrhan took the overall Tour du Rwanda 2023 general classification victory from Italy's Walter Calzoni. This was Eastern Africa's day – an African victory on African soil. President Kagame was on the stage, decorating Mulubrhan with the Tour du Rwanda yellow jersey and other prizes. Then we were asked to stand as the Eritrean national anthem rang out. Following this, a large number of Eritrean cycling fans stood aside the podium stage chanting, 'Henok!!! Henok!!! Henok!!! Henok!!!', demanding attention from their cycling hero.

After a short time back in the pavilion, President Kagame suddenly stood up, and in a split second his bodyguards did the same. Kagame turned, smiled, waved goodbye and walked away to enjoy the rest of his Sunday. The chanting Eritrean cycling fans eventually got hold of their cycling hero and, like a trophy, hoisted him on to their shoulders, draped him in the khedra and awlie flags, and, singing loudly, took him away.

Given his strong experience of winning on African soil, Henok Mulubrhan could well become the next African cycling icon – the 'New Black Cyclone' of the Rwanda 2025 UCI World Championships for road racing. Maybe victory at the 2023 Tour du Rwanda was his dress rehearsal for a future date with destiny. He has some top-quality Eritrean teammates, including Biniam Girmay, Merhawi Kudus, Natnael Berhane and Natnael Tesfatsion. If they are all fit and qualify for the race, then Eritrea will have useful numbers to field a strong African team for the event.

After the Tour du Rwanda I followed up with some of the FERWACY leaders and asked them what they considered would be a strong legacy for the 2025 UCI Road World Championships. What did they hope to achieve for cycling? Benoit Munyankindi said:

'This 2025 World Road Race World Championships being in Rwanda is for us a big achievement as it will be for the first time in Africa . . . We will increase the number of the licensed riders. We will have experience in organising the top event. Rwanda will benefit from this event on all sides. The Rwanda Cycling Federation will also benefit from it [in terms of] equipment and this will help in the future to organise another world-leading race event, not only Tour of Rwanda.'

Pascal Ndizeye Nkunduwite's response was:

'I see the legacy after 2025 World Championships as Rwanda marking its name to the history of the cycling game worldwide, respected across the world. The kids of Rwanda will love the cycling game more than ever before. Hopefully Rwanda will have a good facility for cyclists that will remain here forever.'

While Liliane Kayirebwa said:

'Kigali 2025 will be one of the biggest events ever we will host in Rwanda. This will increase the visibility of Rwanda and it's a privilege to host this big event. We will get more sponsors, partners, through the event and they will bring wealth as well. Different people will get jobs. Hotels, restaurants, bars, the food markets and different domains will gain more money through hosting them. The Rwanda Cycling Federation will get experience of organising big events. We will also get technical experience for the commission, for the riders, technicians and so many people in our cycling family.'

Increasing the number of riders who want to take up the sport; new facilities; greater employment opportunities; the ability to organise future world-leading cycling events – all these are seen as benefits the people of Rwanda will enjoy as a result of hosting the UCI Road World Championships. I felt a champion's heart pounding with desire in the people I met in Rwanda. After the traumatic experiences of the past, and in still healing from this in the present, they are developing cycling for their communities and society, to demonstrating themselves as the world leaders of the sport that they will become in Kigali 2025; defeat for Rwanda is not possible. In representing the sport of cycling, it is Rwanda and its people who will be crowned the kings and queens of world cycling during Kigali 2025. For me, those superb cyclists who are presented with medals and get to wear the UCI rainbow jerseys for their marvellous efforts are going to be the decorative sideshow to something much greater occurring in Africa.

12

Internationale Vélo Force (VIF 2020)

'What are your thoughts about having an international cycling federation, established and led by Black people, for representing the interests of Black cyclists from grassroots to professional across the world, for protecting them from encounters with racism in the sport?' This was the question I put to many Black cyclists in 2020, around the time of the Black Lives Matter anti-racism protests. I did this in relation to thinking about the state of professional cycling in Europe over the years and particularly in response to the amateur, elite and professional Black racing cyclists and riders who in my research for writing my book *Desire, Discrimination, Determination* had shared directly with me accounts of the violent racial discrimination they had encountered, with no form of punishment given to the perpetrators by national and international cycling authorities.

In my further investigations for writing this book, in Chapter 10 Black cyclists from across the African continent including the Kenyan rider Sule Kangangi, the Ugandan rider Charles Kagimu and the Rwandan rider Adrien Niyonshuti shared their testimonies with me about their continued struggles to gain visas to race their bikes internationally due to what they saw as racial profiling. This is in contrast to the ease of passage given to their white peers from Africa. Grassroots Black cyclists from the USA including Malaku 'Prince' Mekonnen, founder of Team Cycling Royalty; Ajoa Abrokwa of She is Fit and Focused from Philadelphia; and Babalola Ajisafe of Century Road Club Association and the Major Taylor Development Cycling Team, as discussed in Chapters 3 and 7 of this book, have shared with me on the racism that they had encountered at recreational events and competitions, away from the safe spaces of their local neighbourhoods, and how they felt threatened when cycling due to the hostility towards them in white-dominated cycling spaces.

During and briefly after the Black Lives Matter protests 'diversity' became a buzzword used by some national cycling bodies, for example in the UK and the USA, and even the UCI. In my view, where there is a call for bettering racial diversity and inclusive cycling, the direct action is through 'anti-racist' messaging, and action in education, policy and in practice. Conversations about 'racism' and 'anti-racism' and these online meetings were occurring between some of the leading elite and professional Black cyclists from across the USA, France, Eritrea and the UK following the Black Lives Matter anti-racism protests of 2020, and during the COVID-19 lockdown period in the same year. I had helped to lead the organisation of online meetings, and included the Black cycling champion riders Grégory Baugé, Kévin Reza, Natnael Berhane, Mark McKay, Justin Williams, Yohann Gène, Ayesha McGowan and Charlotte Cole-Hossain. We were considering creating a Black-led cycling movement to become a collective voice for championing anti-racism and support for Black cyclists, from grassroots riders to professionals, across the world. We had agreed on the name, VIF 2020, by rearranging the initials of Internationale Vélo Force or the

International Bike Force, and were set to launch in November 2020 with a press release:

'The year 2020 will be remembered for the fervent wave of Black Lives Matter protests by people across the world demanding an end to racial violence and all forms of discriminations specifically towards people of African descent. Despite the historical evidence and public cases of racial abuse in the peloton, the cycling industry and leaders have not given attention to the various issues preventing the sport from truly becoming a sport for all. VIF 2020 will endeavour to examine cycling policymaking, practices and actions hindering genuine representation in the sport and help stamp out racism in the cycling world.'

However, despite all the effort we put in, VIF 2020 did not launch, and I saw that our failure to ignite was caused by lack of solid consensus as to who would be most appropriate to lead the group. Would this be an American rider? A French rider? A British rider? A current rider? A retired rider? How committed to the role could any chosen VIF 2020 leader be? I saw not launching VIF 2020 as a missed opportunity to build, present and have some control over the public discourse in cycling on challenging 'racism', particularly given that we were a powerful international collective of Black cycling champions seeking to further the interests of Black people in cycling across the world, but I remained interested in whether there was an appetite for something like VIF 2020 outside the original collective of Black cyclists.

I was particularly interested in the voices of some of the leading African and African-Caribbean cyclists that I had come to know. I found that there was a mixed response from those that I discussed the concept with. For example, the Rwandan cyclist Adrien Niyonshuti did not see anything like VIF 2020 functioning with any tangible influence outside the UCI, saying, 'The UCI are too big an organisation around the world, especially for cycling. If the UCI can work with those people who have engaged with them, we should not cross the barrier. We should work with the UCI.'

A similar, but broader response to discussing the possibilities of working with and within the dominant, white-led powers of world cycling came from the USA rider, 2022 Florida State cycling champion Sheerie Edwards, who said:

'I don't think we need a Black governing body. What we need is the white-dominated governing body to make space. We need Black people at the table and more Black pro team ownership, including Black designers for cycling apparel that caters to the body type of Black people. Just ensuring that there is representation at every level and facet. We have more than enough talent to dominate in the field and continue to make our own mark in the sport.'

When I spoke with the Kenyan cyclist Sule Kangangi before his death, he was positive about such an organisation, particularly to support Black cyclists from Africa on key racism issues. He said:

'I think it is something that would help the sport, as long as it is not extreme. For supporting with visas and for giving a voice about issues we face in the peloton. This can help. For me, myself, I have been in the peloton and people want to call me names. We need to get with the issues behind this.'

Fatima Deborah Conteh, the leading woman cyclist from Sierra Leone, agreed to some degree with the idea of a Black-led world cycling organisation, with an autonomous voice, working with, within and in parallel to the UCI, when she said:

'Our biggest potential dream for a Black-led world organisation is to see that they create awareness to the UCI, to bring more World Tour races to Africa. Also create more logistics support, and especially more racing bikes and recent bicycle components for Africans.'

Concurring with Fatima Deborah Conteh, the Jamaican rider Llori Sharpe said:

'Such an organisation could be great and can certainly empower and stimulate the imaginations and visions of Black people within cycling.

If the organisation's environment remains encouraging and conducive to the growth of the Black presence in cycling, then undoubtedly its potential power would be undeniable.'

When the South African Velokhaya Life Cycling Academy cycling coach and school headteacher Jacob Lempe spoke with me, he took a similar view to Llori Sharpe and shared his opinion on the need for Black leadership in cycling through an organisation that would act as a voice for Black people's empowerment and representation:

'Definitely! There should be an independent Black organisation for Black Africans. These people can be ambassadors for Africans – to create relationships, to create awareness, to respect us. Not just giving white people the opportunity.'

The female USA rider and Black activist cycling leader Ajoa Abrokwa said:

'There is a future for a Black coalition or a Black consortium; a Black governing body or Black authority that convenes to discuss all aspects of the industry and its global direction. This Black body can consist of those leading names in the Black cycling community. There is opportunity at every level to lead cultural shifts that create huge impact. I believe the key is having major stakeholders, strategists, creatives and grassroots leaders meet quarterly to discuss the current landscape and the collective approach to change it.'

Some of the cyclists I spoke to from Africa supported the idea of working with and within the structures of the UCI, so what action has been taken by the national bodies for cycling to create and shape a genuine sense of inclusion, connection and belonging to the sport for all? Since the 2020 Black Lives Matter protests there has been some multi-ethnic engagement from the UK national cycling body, British Cycling. In 2021, they announced their bringing together of 14 experts from a variety of industries and backgrounds, as a Diversity and Inclusion Advisory Group (DIAG) responsible for tracking the organisation's progress against the long-term Diversity and Inclusion Strategic Framework. This is in order to provide advice to the Executive Leadership Team, Board of Directors and British Cycling staff. Interestingly, none of the 14 members were Black people. Some seemed to be of either mixed-heritage or British-Asian background, all others were white people. Framing race together with issues of sex, gender, disability and all other protected characteristics in my view diminishes the power of discrete concentration that each of the protected characteristics deserves for bettering equality, equity and inclusion. Ultimately, periphery activities through the British Cycling DIAG can be taken to provide a discourse of diversity, and to help with administrative box ticking, but the real decision-making and action for the sport remains at the core with a British Cycling Executive Board membership, a group that is dominantly white.

To be fair, following Black Lives Matter some aims for tackling the 'ethnicity gap in the sport' in relation to British Cycling's #OurRide strategy were announced, including 'being more ambitious in our approaches to recruitment by employing from a more diverse talent pool'. This language made it seem as though the mood was changing. Seeing concrete outcomes depends on the sustainability of the vision and how well the mission stands up to political counter challenges such as 'whitelash' and accusations of 'wokeness'.

The rationale behind the #OurRide strategy cites my Made in Britain cycling research project as a key source in its conception. So, on its implementation, I wrote to a British Cycling executive leader asking whether they would like me to provide a solid professional critical academic evaluation of its impact. But she never got back to me on this offer. It is difficult to make a clear sense of the impact of #OurRide strategy, and of the DIAG's influence, if any, on the British Cycling executive board. British Cycling Annual reports of 2023 give information on City Academies being established across the UK for fostering access to the sport through diversity and inclusion. However, in terms of what the general non-cycling public and non-British Cycling members have seen in 2024, an Olympic year in Paris, is that ethnic representation at professional levels of cycling across all the disciplines, particularly in track and road cycling, remains dominantly white, just as this was in 2016 when I began to share with the general public my Made in Britain research project.

In comparison to British Cycling, USACycling, the national body in the USA, were more vocal and active about changing the dominance of whiteness across cycling culture. In 2020, it established a Diversity, Equity and Inclusion (DEI) Task Force with two primary goals: to increase diversity among USACycling board and staff, and to increase diversity in the USA cycling community. USACycling introduced and drove forwards a range of inclusive initiatives, such as the Search for Speed track talent ID programme, which focuses on introducing track cycling to diverse and underrepresented Los Angeles communities and providing Black youth and Black young adults with a dedicated pathway to the USA national cycling team with a view to diversifying ethnic group representation at the Los Angeles Olympic Games in 2028. Time will tell how this works out. In partnership with the Historically Black Colleges and Universities and Tribal Colleges and Universities, USACycling is also developing the collegiate cycling programme. The aim here is to promote diversity, equity and inclusion. The collaborations include working with the cycling technology brand Zwift to host cycling inclusion conferences and promote its Olympic development scholarship to underrepresented (Black) athletes. USACycling has also shaped grassroots community collaborations across New York in partnership with Major Taylor Iron Riders, New York Cycle Club, Equity Design and Free Bikes 4 Kidz to help provide bikes to young Black people.

In the USA at least, Black people in cycling seem to be more represented in working with and within the existing structures of the national bodies. This positioning for shaping change and transformation in the sport connects to some of the responses I received from the racing cyclists across the world that I spoke with. They see that the best place to advance diversity and inclusion and anti-racism in the sport is at the table in the house of the powers that be in cycling. However, I take caution in this from the words of American professor, poet and civil rights activist Audre Lorde, 'The master's tools will never dismantle the master's house. They will never enable us to bring about genuine change.' Diversity and inclusion discourses for Black people in cycling will never cut the power in the house that is sourced and fuelled by whiteness. Invitations to work with some of the national bodies that I have mentioned may aim outwardly in presenting inclusion of 'ethnic' diversity, but with this, those that take up the invite into the house of white power will only ever possibly be able to change some of the aesthetics inside: new furniture, a new paint scheme. My analogy here relates to the redecorated communications of language, visual discourses and temporary time-framed equality, diversity and inclusion projects. In fact, those who have entered these white houses of cycling power for a seat at the table are also providing education to the powers that be on how to become smarter in mitigating any future criticisms made towards them about racial inequities in cycling. These white houses of cycling power will always remain built on the same foundations owned by the master.

I think Black people in cycling need to establish their Internationale Vélo Force. They need to respond as one to the public discourse in cycling on racism and 'anti-racism', and not have this articulated to them by white-led cycling national bodies and organisations across the world. VIF as a powerful collective of Black cyclists can work to enact the interests of Black people across the globe in cycling, functioning without being constrained by the dominant Eurocentric ways of being. This would be an Internationale Vélo Force that is unafraid to choose its own ways of seeing cycling, and acting in the interests of Black people in the sport – from grassroots to professional.

In 2020, I saw VIF as the beginning of a decolonising process for anti-racism in cycling, for addressing the inequitable way in which cycling has been and is presented across the world, and Black people's repositioning of those representations in bringing a collective voice to speak as one. To be fully committed with this original concept means challenging the white-dominated sphere of cycling, including the powers of their national bodies and the UCI by speaking and acting on behalf of Black people in cycling via a solidly organised group. A new and brave collective of international Black cyclists is needed who are prepared to take the original VIF 2020 concept forward, using their own experiences and visions of what they want the culture of their sport to look like.

13

The diasporic turn

On my way home to the UK from Johannesburg, at the bookshop in Oliver Tambo International Airport, I noticed a book called *Ubuntu for Warriors* by Colin Chasi. I knew 'ubuntu' as an ancient African 'moral code' meaning 'humanity to others' and defined as 'I am what I am because of who we all are', but as I skimmed through the book, I was drawn by a subversive interpretation of ubuntu 'for warriors' in discussion of the leadership and influence on people in their liberation given by South African figures of warfare and peace such as King Shaka, Nelson Mandela, Desmond Tutu, Winnie Madikizela-Mandela, Kenneth

Kaunda and Steve Biko. Chasi says, 'Africans need to know how, when, why, and to what end their warriors are leashed and unleashed in small and great fights for more just social orders.' In presenting ubuntu over the generations through these great South African leaders, it can be seen how, in times of warfare and peace, the ubuntu warrior is a champion of social justice for the transformation of humanity.

After talking with the Sierra Leonean woman cyclist Fatima (Deborah) Conteh about the struggles she faced achieving her cycling dream, I offered to form a cycling team around her and suggested we call it Team Ubuntu. I shared my interpretations of the term with her and suggested that we build the team specifically for African women cyclists and begin with the inaugural all-women's cycling team in Sierra Leone. The presence of this team at racing events, and the victories that would hopefully follow, would be enough to make public statements about our purpose. I saw that with Deborah's racing experience, her desire and determination, we could develop and present this concept of African women as role models in cycling. We took this forward.

I had understood from sources in some African countries about the difficult challenges faced by young African women in some sports, including cycling. Women are often prevented by men from cycling and pursuing their ambitions in the sport. I was told by one person, 'Women as cycling athletes are seen as idle and time-wasting.' Even worse, in some cases it has been alleged that they have then been harassed by men for sexual favours in return for advancement in the sport. And in all of this, the national federations' lack of will to fully investigate complaints of sexual harassment in showing accountability to the welfare of women cyclists, it is the young women making the claims of sexual harassment who face being suspended or banned from the sport, not the sexual predators they are accusing. I had understood that many young women have quit cycling because of this and are fearful to speak out about it.

These experiences of African women in sport are no different to those faced by young women across the globe in sport. For example, in 2022,

30 sexual abuse allegations were made against British Gymnastics as part of a UK investigation. Many complaints focused on physical and emotional abuse. It was said that a culture of silence and a gymnast's reliance on their coaches meant complaints were hard to make, and, if problems were raised, the processes to deal with them often failed. In the USA, women's soccer was accused of having 'an extensive and widespread culture of sexual and emotional abuse'. A former US deputy attorney general heading the investigation found that abuse and sexual misconduct were 'systemic in the sport, at all levels of participation, from the pros to the youth level'. In August 2023, the president of the Spanish football federation, Luis Rubiales, was widely criticised for kissing footballer Jenni Hermoso on the lips following Spain's 1-0 victory over England in the World Cup final in Sydney, Australia. Rubiales said the player had consented, but Hermoso rejected this as 'categorically false'. After three weeks of intense public scrutiny, Rubiales finally quit as head of Spain's football federation.

When I was a primary school teacher, also focused on establishing and building my cycling teams, I was always proud of my riders, the female riders especially who went on to win many individual and team national schools championships. I felt that I could do the same with the young women that would be recruited by Deborah and myself to race for Team Ubuntu. Given the lack of exposure of many African women's cycling teams compared to the norm of men's teams, I wanted to sponsor and bring together a small team to represent women as champions of the sport. So, Team Ubuntu – 'for women cycling warriors' as I named it – was about empowering young African women to recognise their abilities and ambitions, and their sense of female cultural creativity, and for challenging gender discrimination. In my view, the existence of Team Ubuntu would say:

'We love riding our bikes. No one will stop us. We are here. Beautiful, Black and beautiful. We look towards the possibilities across Africa in fulfilment of our cycling journeys. There are millions of African women like us across the continent. We can inspire, connect and create our joys of cycling across Africa through our own defined ubuntu cycling style.'

Team Ubuntu – Sierra Leone

Team Ubuntu was conceived as a 'sankofa', through the lenses of my diasporic turn to Africa, as a Black-British man of African-Caribbean ethnic group origins. The 'sankofa' *'Se wo were fi na wosan kofa a yenkyiri'* from the Akan Tribe of Ghana is a proverb which means to learn from the past, and to take those riches for use in the present and possible future, to 'go back and get it.'

In the UK, the British-Nigerian cyclist Temi Lateef, leader of London's Black Riders Association, often uses his Instagram account to narrate his biennial bike ride from London to Lagos, Nigeria, and raise broader awareness of the popular BMX cycling scene across the African city. The Philadelphia cycling groups Kings Rule Together (KRT) and Queens Rule Together (QRT) have also shared accounts of their cycling touring experiences across Ghana. Of this, they wrote:

'KRT and QRT made its way to the Motherland. That's right, we were cycling in Africa! This was our second time taking an international trip as a club and by far one of the most humbling experiences of our lives. Cycle Ghana's itinerary was loaded with things for us to do. We cycled 50+ miles through some of Ghana's most historic sites. Our first stop was to the Cape Coast Castle, one of about 40 slave castles built on the Gold Coast of West Africa. It's a castle, indeed, but not like the ones we read about in fairytales. It was a slave-trade outpost from the late 17th century to the early 19th century. During this time, millions of Africans were forced on to slave ships bound for the United States. Our tour guide, leaving no detail untold, watched us as we tried to wrap our heads around the experience. The feelings we felt, in that moment, will never be forgotten.'

The former USA professional cyclist Rahsaan Bahati appears to have taken the diasporic turn to Africa too, in what seems to be in the spirit of ubuntu. Bahati journeyed to Accra, Ghana, in 2023 with his charitable foundation for the Ride to New Horizons African Cycling Initiative. This is a cycling development partnership with the Ghanian Cycling Federation, the Gladiators Cycling Club of Accra, the Burkina Faso Cycling Federation and the University of Ouagadougou Cycling Team based in Burkina Faso. Together they support young aspirant cyclists preparing for possible selection to race at the 2025 UCI Road World Championships in Rwanda and at the 2028 Olympic Games cycling events in California, USA. When the Ghanian rider Farrakhan Shaaban Mohammed took victory at the youth category Derbywheel National Tour Du Ghana event in September 2023, he pointed to the immediate impact of this new international collaboration with the African diaspora, saying, 'I am very happy and enthusiastic about the Bahati Foundation's collaboration, and the MOU with the Ghana Cycling Federation will assist the youth towards the upcoming African Games in Ghana.'

I'd been following how Ghana has been working to raise the profile of its national and international cycling events, and I discussed this with Conteh. She had contacted me with a plan in relation to this. She wanted to lead Team Ubuntu for two races in Accra, Ghana, during September 2023: the Pru Ride and the Osagyefo Criterium. She had thought out how she could win the races, along with the prize fund available, and be able to return to Sierra Leone with her prized road bike, which had been retained by bag handlers at the international airport in Accra during her visit to the country some months earlier, due to it being overweight for the flight. Deborah had used that steel bicycle earlier on in the year in Ghana and with success at the Ride Afrique international criterium, where she debuted the Team Ubuntu jersey and achieved second place in a field packed with strong riders from Ghana and Nigeria. I liked her ambition and confidence about the Pru Ride and the Osagyefo Criterium.

One evening, when I was scrolling through Facebook and a Grass Track Cycling Group, I came across the work of Vida Juliet Vivie, a pioneering woman cyclist and cycling advocate from the Peki-Avetile region of Ghana. I was fascinated by how she had developed the grass track cycling racing discipline into a cycling programme for young people. I was curious to know more about her, as this was also a racing discipline that I had dipped my toe into from time to time during my own bike racing career. I got in touch with Vida.

In our conversation, she told me that her father, John Green Kwame Vivie, was a keen cyclist and photographer, and also her mentor, and that he was the first person to use a road bike in their rural Ghanian community. John Green used to set his bike on a stand and pedal this to generate power to print his photographs. He was also a dedicated bicycle repairer, repairing bicycles for the local people. I asked Vida about cycling opportunities for girls and women in Ghana, past and present, and whether there was any sort of legacy or current developments in place apart from her own. She said, 'I did not do any cycling racing myself. Ghana did not have a plan to introduce girls into cycling sport, nor organise races for women. Ghana did not organise women's cycling as a sport, but I have done numerous cycling tours as an individual myself.'

I saw that by giving young women access to the sport through her version of grass track cycling racing, Vida was enacting ubuntu for social justice, seeking transformation in a male-dominated Ghanian cycling culture. She told me that her aim in running an entry-level grass track racing event was to get more girls into racing, and that about 3000 young women and girls have been through her cycling programme.

I came up with a collaborative idea for Vida and Team Ubuntu. I suggested that we put together some of the young women riders she was working with and team up with Deborah as an international Team Ubuntu – in Ghana. We agreed to make this happen. All of this momentum presented me with the opportunity to travel to Ghana to meet with Team Ubuntu, and to work with Vida on piloting my teacher education cycling for schools programme in the Peki-Avetile region. This would be working with teachers and young children at their schools, fostering the possibility of using cycling in the curriculum for physical education. Deborah arrived in Ghana the week before I did. She met with Vida and her two young protégés, named Rebecca and Hannah, still both at school, but with whom she would form Team Ubuntu for the races ahead.

Deborah had led them in some training rides in and around Peki-Avetile just days before the Pru Race in Accra. When this race came, Deborah finished in seventh place and was not happy. The race motorbikes had cut through her racing line, on many occasions causing her to fall and lose touch with the leading break of riders. This was a similar story to her experiences at the Ride Afrique earlier on in the year, but she'd managed to stay upright in that one. Rebecca and Hannah, as novice riders making their racing debuts in an elite women's race, both managed to finish. Everything was new for them. In fact, this was the first time that they had ever visited their country's capital city, Accra.

I travelled to Ghana to meet Vida, Deborah and the team at the Osagyefo Criterium. This is a cycling race named for Dr Kwame Nkrumah, who led his people to independence from British colonial rule and in 1960 became Ghana's first president. In achieving this, he was hailed as 'Osagyefo', which means redeemer in the Akan language. Dr Nkrumah is known for coining the term 'neo-colonialism'. This is a theory that defines a dependent, paternalistic relationship between post-colonial African countries and their former colonial European powers. Politically, Dr Nkrumah was a Pan-Africanist, an ideology taken by various movements in Africa and the African diaspora, past and present, that have as their common goal the unity of Africans, and the elimination of colonialism and white supremacy from the continent.

I had arrived in Accra the night before and at 7.30 a.m. the next day the temperature had already reached 24 degrees Celsius. It was going to be a hot day. I travelled by taxi from my hotel in the Cantonment area to meet Vida and the Team Ubuntu riders, Rebecca and Hannah, who themselves had set off at 4 a.m. from Peki-Avetile, travelling by car to Accra. Fortunately for me, the taxi journey was just a short hop away from the race event's start and finish area, and very much a straight drive through Accra's own Oxford Street. The recognisable names of British colonial rule gave way to names associated with uprising and liberation when the driver turned off Oxford Street and on to 28 February Road. This was the site of the Accra uprisings which occurred on 28 February 1948. The uprising is said to have begun as a peaceful protest march by unarmed former soldiers, veterans of World War II, who had fought with the Gold Coast Regiment of the Royal West African Frontier Force. They were calling out the British governor to respect and deliver on his promise of post-war pension benefits. However, the march was broken up by police and violence erupted, leaving three leaders of the protest march dead. The incident is viewed as 'the straw that broke the camel's back' and marks the key point in the political process of the Gold Coast becoming the first African colony to achieve independence – it became Ghana on 6 March 1957.

The taxi driver drove on. Then, in front of me, the imposing sight of the enormous Independence Arch and the Black Star Gate Square, decorated with Ghanaian flags – red, gold and green with a black star at the centre. I felt that I had been taken to a space of ubuntu, a historic African space of Black liberation to be remembered in the everyday present as one where social justice and transformation were actualised through Black revolution.

I climbed out of the taxi just outside of the national sports stadium. I wandered in, but I could not see anybody around who looked like they could help, or any sign of an event headquarters, so I wandered back out of the stadium area and on to the roadside. My mobile phone rang. It was Vida, who directed me to where she was. I shared with her what I'd seen on my journey and asked about Dr Nkrumah – what did he mean to people today? She replied, 'Oh! Our best president! Our best! He did so much for the people. Our best president.' Vida's enthusiasm in talking about Dr Nkrumah provided me with the sense of his interminable iconic status for Ghanian people.

The Osagyefo Criterium was organised by Gladiators Cycling Team of Accra. Vida introduced me to Emmanuel Antwi, one of the race founders, who was in charge of race organisation. He told me that Gladiators Cycling Team had created the event in order to contribute to the promotion and improvement of competitive cycling in Africa, and that this was the third edition of the event. I looked around. It was a Thursday morning. I wondered how they would be able to run a bike race on a mid-week morning, with only a few roads closed, but Emmanuel reassured me:

'Today is a bank holiday to honour the birthday of our great president. We always have other African riders from different African countries in the race, especially from West Africa. Today there will be lots of riders from Nigeria here, adding to the spirit of unity and helping strengthen the competitive nature of the race among the athletes. The numbers coming today will speak to the popularity of the event; the numbers being the sheer number of registrants and the number of award positions, especially for the female category, and of course, the spectators.'

One by one, street merchants began to appear; some selling second-hand cycling shoes; some selling fresh coconut milk from the coconuts loaded on their carts; traders head-carrying their loads of cold drinks for sale. In between all this, the race competitors began to appear in groups and as individuals from both directions of the Startlets 91 Road start and finish line, which was closed to traffic. Indeed, Emmanuel was true to his word. The event had attracted some of the strongest riders from across Western Africa, including the 2023 women's African Continental Road Champion, Ese Lovina Ukpeseraye of the Nigerian national cycling team.

Ese Lovina Ukpeseraye

Conteh arrived, reacquainted with her white and blue steel Viner racing bicycle, wearing her pink Team Ubuntu jersey, her hair in long braids. She introduced me to some of the cyclists from Ghana, including Frank Quaye, a young aspirant elite racer who had had experiences of racing in the Tour de Faso stage race in Burkina Faso. As we were talking, several other riders came over to introduce themselves as Instagram followers, including Foster Doevi of Ghana and Henry Odumu of Nigeria.

Following a ceremonial lap of the race route led by a member of the Gladiators Cycling Team in recognition of Osagyefo, the racers took to the start line. It was only 10 a.m., but it was close to 30 degrees Celsius and the heat from the sun was kicking in. I had to get back to my hotel to check out and get my luggage as we were heading off straight after to race to Peki-Avetile with Vida to carry out some work for my cycling for schools project, but I stayed around to see the beginning of the race and to wave off Team Ubuntu.

The race began at the sound of the foghorn. First the male riders departed. Three minutes later, the female riders were off. I hung around for a while, but there was no large race screen or commentary to help with tracking the riders, so I headed off to take a taxi to my hotel. As I walked on up the Startlets 91 Road, an early break from the men's race began to flash by. Then the chasing peloton followed. At the Kinbu Road and Liberia Road junction, a marshal was ready. He stopped the traffic to wave the riders through, but it was not so good for the dropped riders, who had to jump the lights at the road junction and then weave their way through cars and lorries attempting to recover their race position in the peloton. I looked ahead towards the Libera Road at what appeared to be the men's peloton racing with and through the flow of Accra morning traffic.

On my return from the hotel with my luggage, I walked up the side of Startlets 91 Road towards the start/finish line area. Among the spectators I spotted Vida. She was sat with Conteh, who looked miserable. 'What happened?' I said. 'Are you OK?' She pointed to her wheels and pressed both the tyres. 'I get two flats.' She had aborted the race. She looked on with a thousand-mile stare of misery. Both her front and rear tyres were blown, the back wheel, buckled. 'The road surface is not good. The potholes. No spare wheels.' This was a disappointing race for Deborah. However, Rebecca and Hannah were still involved. Each of them were riding solo efforts as novice riders in their second-ever elite bike race, having been caught out by the furious pace that was set early on. Eventually, the women's race was won with a powerful sprint by Ese Lovina Ukpeseraye. The men's race was won by Foster Doevi of the Gladiators Cycling Team to huge shouts of joy from the spectators.

Waiting for the podium ceremony was a long, drawn-out process in the intense heat of the Accra afternoon sun. The race organisers invited me to present some awards, which I did. Following this, I got talking to Doevi, Frank Quaye and Henry Odumu about the race, their racing and their experiences of the sport in their respective countries. This was a really interesting and insightful conversation, and I learned more about what they, as elite West African cyclists, saw as the barriers and opportunities in cycling, and what their ambitions were going forwards. I was particularly curious to find out from them why I hadn't regularly come across West Africans on the world stage, on the track or on the road. Foster Doevi began:

'Elite racing in Ghana is very competitive. Every team wants to be at the top due to the work they put into training. During elite races there is no friendship, because everyone belongs to a team and listens to their team captain and follows the team plan. I think West Africa men have not yet made huge breakthroughs in European cycling, because most West African countries are inadequate in good training and coaches and lack tools and equipment.'

I sensed that this was going to get some very frank responses when Henry Odumu nodded at this in relation to Nigeria:

'Yes, it's really competitive. The guys in Nigeria are very strong with great motivations. Each and every one of us have something we're good at; some are good in duathlon, triathlon and normal crits [criteriums]. The reason why we the West Africans have not made any

huge breakthroughs in European cycling is because of corruption, lack
of competitions, and not having been exposed to foreign activities.'

I was interested to know what Odumu meant by 'corruption', but at the
same time I felt slightly awkward asking him directly, but then he added:

'There are so many barriers to develop as a cyclist in Nigeria. First of all,
I will train and get stronger, but then, when it comes to international
competitions, the selection processes can be vague to go and represent
the country. If you are the favourite, it is likely you will be chosen. The
pathway in cycling for men in Nigeria is really difficult, so when we're
out competing with the foreigners we hardly place in good positions.'

Doevi agreed, saying, 'Yes. There are not enough races in Ghana. We
need more organisation of these,' and Frank Quaye added, 'We need
more races in Ghana for the riders to race consistently enough. If we
had more races, then our racing levels of experience would rise. We need
more sponsorships for this.'

Financial investment is required to advance coaching knowledge and
provide resources for cyclists at their elite level to be able to compete
equitably as part of the structures in their countries, but this support
is just not there. Doevi and Odumu were not just pure racing cyclists,
they were multi-sport athletes who would also compete as runners and
swimmers in duathlon and triathlons, particularly given the 'lack of
competitions' in cycle racing. In their context, they had to think more
broadly about how to retain their race fitness and competitive edge.

The call for more racing opportunities was clear in all the cyclists'
responses. I asked what they thought about the new interest in African
cycling coming from cycling individuals and groups in the UK and USA,
and how could it help them in the future. Doevi said:

'Cyclists and cycling groups have been arriving from other parts of the
world, such as USA, UK to their motherland [West Africa], to build
cycling relationships. It is good to build new relationships, because it
brings opportunities to share plans and aims, and also build trust for
opportunities in order to gain things we can afford from them.'

I shared some of my thoughts about the UCI Road World Championships in Kigali in 2025 and asked them whether they believed an African rider could win and become a UCI World Champion. Surprisingly, they were confident that there would be an African winner, one day in the future, when Africans and Europeans had equal access to cycling resources, but they seemed to accept that cycling was a global game, that the inequality between wealthier European cyclists and poorer Black African cyclists wouldn't change, and that they just had to live with it. There was nothing that they could do about it. I understood this was the way they felt when Foster Doevi said:

'I believe there will be an African winner one day if the best equipment is being provided . . . Bikes, chains, tyre – when all this is being provided African cyclists will try their best to podium, but the winners will always be Europeans, because they have good programmes in their country. They don't really lack anything. They do cycling as their profession and they get paid for it. They have good equipment and tools, such as good bikes, good roads, good managers, good organisation and nutritional values.'

Henry Odumu was even more confident about a positive result for Africans in 2025, when he told me that 'there will be an African winner at the World Championship' in Rwanda in 2025.

What I got from this trio of riders was a genuine understanding of the lived experiences of aspirant elite male West African riders. I tried to put myself in their position, to see the sport from their view, and of course a lot of it made sense. If I were an ambitious young racing cyclist, aiming for the top, dreaming of cycling in Europe, but without much support, the challenges would be huge. In a cycling context I would be poverty-stricken, with a lack of knowledge about cutting-edge coaching to improve my training, a lack of competitions for my growth and development, and a perception that the sporting authorities which are supposed to be supporting me are corrupt. When seeing how cycling in Europe is presented on the television, I see all the glitz and glamour of the Tour de France, the superstars, and I see my fellow sportspeople in football over here in Ghana or in Nigeria making the transition to

Europe, to play in the Premier League for Arsenal or Manchester City. Biniam Girmay got there with cycling, so it can't be an illusion. The dream must be possible and certainly nothing is happening for me here. I asked the guys if they had any ambitions to ever race in Europe and Doevi said:

'I have ambitions to race in Europe. I have developed my hard work and training. In Europe there are more races out there which can help you develop faster and learn new things. Also, in Europe you can improve your hard work. During races you will eat good and get proper treatment and better facilities.'

Henry's words were very much the same:

'Yeah! I have an ambition to race in Europe, seeing how they do their thing makes me want to go there and race with the best. I just believe one day I will get there with the hard work I put into my cycling career.'

We could have talked for longer, but I had to get going. There was a great post-race camaraderie among the riders from Nigeria and Ghana, and across the genders. I caught up with Deborah before I left. She told me of the commitment to the race given by some of the riders from Nigeria who had ridden 450 kilometres to Accra from Lagos a few days before the race as a warm-up and were riding back to Lagos tomorrow. I told her about the possibility of me coming to Sierra Leone later in the year to direct a short training camp for our Team Ubuntu riders who were looking to do well in the Freetown Criterium Classic that was being organised by the Flames Cycling Club of Freetown.

I squeezed my cases into the back seats of Vida's little white car and then squashed myself into the corner to sit with Rebecca and Hannah. We began our drive through the traffic of central Accra to rural Peki-Avetile for the cycling for schools project that I would lead. It was a long journey and it took us along what seemed to be one straight road out of Accra. The only stops we made were at various police checkpoints and garages to tighten up the bolts on the wheel above which I sat.

We had arranged to work with 40 schoolchildren and for me to lead them through a range of activities and skills for racing, including road, track and cyclo-cross, similar to what I had brought to Velokhaya in South Africa. I brought the coaching resources and Vida supplied the bikes, which ranged from BMX to mountain bikes, from youth to adult sizes. All of them had been refurbished by Vida. The school at Peki-Avetile was surrounded by lush green trees and positioned on a hill, just above the local community church. There was a wonderful mountainous landscape in the background. On entering the classroom space, I was introduced by Vida to the headteacher, Mr Sefadzi. The children sat patiently in rows as I introduced myself and then I brought them outside to begin the activities.

It was clear that many had never ridden a bike before in their lives, but those children who had not were determined to prove to their peers that they were natural cyclists. The novelty of the cycling programme caught the eye of local people who lived next to the school. Traders appeared from out of nowhere, head-carrying their loads of cold drinks for sale. Spectators from the nearby houses came over to watch the children riding. After a few skills activities, I could see by the change of light and approaching grey clouds that the weather was going to switch and when a huge wind blew, I halted the programme. Heavy rain then began to fall. We hung around inside and outside under shelter, and then eventually had lunch. Although the rain eased it didn't fully stop, but the children wanted more and I couldn't refuse them, so I called them out into the warm rain. They flew out of the classroom on to their bikes. After some epic cyclo-cross races on a made-up course that I created across the school's football pitch and grass verges, Vida and I handed out certificates to all participants. I felt the programme was a success.

Greater investment and development of cycling for schools programmes as training camps in rural communities were recommended by many of the people that I spoke with during the sharing and implementation of my programme with Velokhaya in South Africa, and my work in

Ghana was to test whether there may be a similar enthusiasm for this. Mr Sefadzi, the headteacher of the school in Peki-Avetile, told me, 'This training should be replicated in all rural communities across Ghana. This will create awareness of opportunities for rural students to carve a career from sporting events, especially cycling.'

Developing cycling opportunities in Ghana for young children was an approach endorsed by Foster Doevi and Henry Odumu in my conversation with them in Accra. Doevi said, 'Children want to see, to turn them to cycling. When there's motivation in the sports environment, and when tools and equipment are being provided, they will put up their possible best to achieve their goals in cycling.' Odumu said, 'To develop young ones into cycling as the sport they love is to give them proper training camps, competitions, taking them across the continent, get them exposed. That alone will turn them to cycling.'

In fostering the cycling for schools teacher education programme in Ghana, in South Africa before this, and in Sierra Leone and Rwanda afterwards, I was educating and providing all teachers that I had met with knowledge that I had learned about cycling over the years – as a racer, and as an educator in promoting opportunities for school education and community development at the grassroots level of the sport. Financial investment and growth in the grassroots of cycling through the coaching of younger children and the professional development of their school teachers across the regions through programmes like mine is also where the skills for racing in cyclo-cross, mountain bike and track cycling can be learned and developed, and future talent spotted.

While I was in Accra, some of the riders told me that in December 2022 the building of a $60 million US dollars indoor track cycling velodrome and multi-sports activity venue, to be paid for by South Korean private investors, had been approved by the government. This is an enormous initiative for West African cycling and a huge investment in track cycling that could develop aspirant track cyclists and attract some of the best track riders from across the continent, and possibly even around the globe, to Ghana. However, in my view this investment will benefit the minority over the majority. Those people in Ghanaian society with the finance to fund their privileged track cycling pursuits are more likely to use the velodrome than, say, the rural children that I worked with in

Peki-Avetile. The better long-term solution in my view would be to use the $60 million investment to create and to sustain a grassroots cycling culture across the country, to build community cycling hubs that include outdoor velodromes or closed circuit tracks which can offer training and racing through a variety of cycling disciplines, such as mountain biking, cyclo-cross, gravel racing or even grass track cycling, the latter of which provides foundational racing skills that could lead to cyclists taking up hard-track indoor velodrome racing in the future.

On my return from Peki-Avetile to central Accra, the traffic was horrendous. I later understood that the police had blocked off the road adjacent to Jubilee House, the residency of President Nana Akufo-Addo, because of three consecutive days of public demonstrations voicing discontent over the rising cost of living and worsening economic conditions. I remembered what Vida told me when I asked her about the legacy of Dr Nkrumah, but since Dr Nkrumah's government was overthrown in 1966, Ghana's severe debt crisis has caused it to take out 17 loans from the International Monetary Fund. This puts Ghana in a position of economic dependency, to the detriment of its growth as an independent nation. No doubt President Nana Akufo-Addo and those in power before him, including Dr Nkrumah, should be held responsible for this crisis, but I see the same economic relationship and paternalistic knowledge dependency reflected in cycling. The desire of African cyclists to mimic the European system isn't going to work for them as it's not a level-playing field.

The 2023 UCI World Championships in Glasgow demonstrated how the sport has been designed in favour of European and white cycling nations. These two weeks of the inaugural multi-disciplined cycling competition presented a self-gratifying Eurocentric utopian stage show in reifying the Eurocentric imagination of excellence across the disciplines of cycling. This Eurocentric vision of world cycling is not equitable in providing genuine inclusion for equality of representation and opportunity for Black people's success, only for their making up the numbers and giving a visual sense of diversity. Some of the more unusual cycling disciplines on display such as Artistic Cycling, Cycle-Ball and Trials were totally populated by white cyclists (generally from Western Europe). I didn't see any Black cyclists involved at all. At the end of Glasgow 2023, in the final outcome, apart from a solitary silver medal won by Nicholas Paul of Trinidad and Tobago in the men's track sprint event, Black people from African and Caribbean nations were shamefully absent from both the cycling and paracycling medal tables.

I would like to think that for Black people from Africa and of the African diaspora who are involved in cycling there is much for them to conceive and create together. Applying the power of Dr Nkrumah's imagination of Pan-Africanism and African unity through Chasi's notion of ubuntu can perhaps support with thinking about beholding, enacting and sustaining a revolutionary Afrocentric vision for their own cycling utopias. This would be in resistance to the neo-colonial habitus that is being reproduced through the magnetic pull and influence of the European imagination of cycling excellence.

14

New Black Cyclones

Grégory Baugé of France – a multiple world track sprint cycling champion – is the only recognisable Black professional track sprint cyclist that has been able to make the transition from athlete to national coach in Europe. Baugé's influence in leading the French national track sprint team has enabled some outstanding Black track sprint cycling athletes to emerge, such as Taky Marie-Divine Kouamé and Melvin Landerneau racing for *Les Bleus* as World and European champions. Baugé's force as the Black Cyclone of his time was an exception to the norm of white athlete dominance in the sport, and is similar to the original Black Cyclone that came before him – Marshall 'Major' Taylor.

Exceptional multiple World Championship-winning Black cycling athletes like Taylor and Baugé interacting at elite and professional level in European and World track cycling have been rare occurrences. There aren't many on the horizon either. When I looked at rider representation at the 2022 UCI World Junior Track Championships held in Tel Aviv, Israel, this presented a clear pattern of what is likely to be European national and white rider dominance for years to come through the next generation of world-leading track cyclists. It's important to present the full extent of this to show the racial exclusivity in the sport. Of the junior team sprint for women, the only non-white team was Korea. There were no national teams from the Caribbean or Africa. In the junior team sprint for men, the only team from Africa was South Africa, but all riders in this team were white people: Michael Jervis, Jordan September and Matthew Lester. The only non-white team was from Korea. This pattern was repeated in event after event, from the junior scratch race to the Keirin.

When looking at the women's junior scratch race, there were some national teams from Asia, such as Japan, and Hong Kong China, but there were no teams or riders representing nations from the dominant Black people nations of the Caribbean or from Africa. Looking at the women's junior team pursuit event was similar. The only non-white team in participation was from Japan. Again, there were no teams representing the dominant Black people nations of the Caribbean and the African continent. In the men's junior team pursuit, there was a team from Argentina, and the only other non-European national team was from South Africa. All riders in that team were white people. When looking at the women's junior sprint, five from the 16 qualifiers to the match sprint rounds came from non-European countries including India, Colombia, Trinidad and Tobago, and two riders from Korea. However, there was no Black African representation in the competition. In the men's junior keirin, 11 of the 30 riders in total came from non-European countries. This included two riders from India. There was just one rider from the Caribbean – Trinidad and Tobago. There were no Black riders at all from Africa in the field. The women's junior elimination race fielded a majority of riders of European descent. There were no riders present from the dominant Black people nations of Africa or the Caribbean. In the men's junior sprint, of the 34 riders, there was just one rider from the Caribbean – Devante Laurence of Trinidad and Tobago. The field did include two riders from Africa, and they were both white people from South Africa. The women's junior omnium had riders in general of European descent, and there were no riders in this event from the dominant Black people nations of the Caribbean and Africa. When looking at the men's junior individual pursuit, there were no riders involved from the Caribbean. The riders were generally of European nations, and Africa's only representation in this event came from two white South African riders. This was mirrored in the men's junior points race. Again, this consisted of 24 riders in total, with no riders representing the Caribbean. Africa's only representation was from one white South African rider. In the men's junior omnium, there were 24 riders in total, a majority being from European nations. There were no riders present from the Caribbean. Africa's only representation was from one white South African rider. For the women's junior individual pursuit, out of the 28 riders in total, there were no riders representing the dominant Black people nations of the Caribbean or from Africa. The event consisted generally of riders of European descent. The men's junior elimination race had majority riders of European descent. The women's junior keirin had 17 riders, but none from Africa. There was just one rider from the Caribbean, Phoebe Sandy of Trinidad and Tobago. The men's junior kilometre time trial event had eight riders. But there were no riders representing the dominant Black people nations of the Caribbean or from Africa. All riders were representing European nations. The women's junior madison had 18 teams in the event. But this race had no teams from the dominant Black people nations of the Caribbean or from Africa. Generally, all riders were of European nations.

There are clear patterns of divide in international track cycling competitions between white-peopled nations across the world and the Black-peopled nations of the Caribbean and the African continent, the exception being South Africa, a nation dominated by Black people, but totally represented by its white minority. There was greater rider representation from some Asian nations, such as Japan and India, than the Caribbean nations. Still, the number of Asian riders was very low in comparison to the number of riders from European and white people dominated nations. This pattern of young white cyclists dominating at the UCI World Junior Track Championships is likely to prevail for some time to come.

I wanted to understand more about the experiences of aspirant young Black track cyclists from African and Caribbean nations. I reached out to Tachana Dalger, the Surinamese National Champion track sprinter. She was 10 years old when she started cycling through a school programme. She told me that she loved sprinting, so was asked by her coach to have a go at track cycling:

> 'I am the only one in my family that rides bikes. There is no history of this in my family. My coach brought me to the Trinidad Easter Grand Prix every year for racing. I first raced on the velodrome in Trinidad when I was aged 17. My biggest win was the Caribbean Championships in 2022, in the 500 metres sprint. I took the gold ahead of Dahlia Palmer from Jamaica.'

I asked her about her ambitions to race at the UCI World Championships or the Olympic Games and she said:

> 'I've tried to get into [the] UCI World Cycling Centre in Switzerland, but could not get in. I have tried hard to seek out sponsorships, but it has been tough, and I haven't achieved any. I have a small bit of Olympic funding to try to qualify for the Olympic Games for 2024.'

When I spoke with Tachana, she was resident in Trinidad and Tobago, the only country in the entire Caribbean region with an indoor velodrome. She said:

> 'It's the only place. There are no other velodromes. I couldn't stay in Suriname. To qualify for the Olympics, I need to gain UCI points. But there are not enough UCI Class 1 competitions in the Caribbean region for this, so this makes it hard to get the points, particularly if you have not the funding to travel so much outside of the region to the races where the most points are on offer.'

Tachana Dalger

It's a tough proposition for Caribbean-based riders like Tashana to fulfil their cycling dreams, but I had a thought. Suriname is a former colony of the Netherlands, the European nation with a supreme cycling pedigree, particularly in track sprinting, and with multiple world-famous indoor velodromes, so I asked Tachana whether there had been any interest from them that she knew of, to support Surinamese people in track cycling. She said, 'No!'

The comparisons of rider representation by nation that I saw at the UCI World Junior Track Cycling Championships in 2022 were pretty much the same as what was on display at the 2023 UCI World Track Championships for senior riders in Glasgow, where there was absolute European dominance in the victory spoils. Great Britain led the way with nine medals – five golds, three silvers and one bronze. Out of the 17 nations that entered, only two of these were from the Global South: Colombia, and Trinidad and Tobago. Each won medals in the men's sprint disciplines. No African nations featured at all in the competition or on the 2023 UCI World Track Championships medal table.

There are stark inequities in track cycling resources across the world that give the absolute advantage of power, representation and success, and a conveyor belt to future development, to riders from European and dominant, white-peopled nations. In the UK there are five 250 metres indoor velodromes in Glasgow (Scotland), Newport (Wales), Derby, Manchester and London (all in England). In Australia there are six: Perth, Thornbury, Melbourne, Sydney, Chandler and Adelaide. Both the UK and Australia each have five times more indoor velodromes for developing Olympic and UCI World Championship track cycling expertise than the entire 54 countries of the African continent. In fact, there is just one indoor velodrome in the whole of the African continent – in Cape Town, South Africa. I wasn't able to visit the venue when I was in Cape Town, but I asked Sipho Mona, manager of Velokhaya Cycling Academy in Cape Town, more about it and he told me, 'It is used and run by Western Province Cycling. It is easily accessible and mostly inclusive when it comes to events, but it's hardly used, and there was a petition to renovate it and the people voted against it because of the costs.'

Voting against the renovation is a huge shame. Access and sustained use of this cycling space can become a great determiner in the narrative of Black cyclists' possible increased representation and success on the UCI and Olympic world stage. Of course, with huge financial costs in building such cycling resources, some African countries may feel it better to invest in their schools and hospitals, rather than in the winning of track cycling medals.

One possible way to create and represent world track cycling as more inclusive and recognisably equitable for all cycling nations across the globe is by raising the profile of competitive grass track oval racing across African nations. This racing discipline has been popular across the UK for over 150 years, with various National Championship events in distances from 400 metre sprints to 5km and 8km endurance racing for men and women. Grass track cycling racing is known in many parts of the Caribbean too, such as Trinidad and Tobago, and Barbados. It is certainly one of the purest forms of bike racing, with no need for investment in huge indoor velodromes that can seat 20,000 spectators and more. All that is needed for grass track cycling racing is a playing field on which racing ovals can be created, track bikes and cyclists ready to compete in events similar to those of indoor velodrome track cycling.

Maybe some of the leaders of world track cycling would see a new focus on competitive grass track cycling as a regressive move, backtracking on the technological advancements of indoor velodrome racing. However, indoor velodrome racing remains fundamentally exclusive to the wealthier European and Asian nations, whereas grass track cycling is inclusive of all cycling nations across the world and at low cost. I do not think that it would be difficult to build, manage and sustain multiple grass track venues across the African and Caribbean cycling nations. Creating this culture at grassroots would offer potential access to millions of new young Black racing cyclists. This could also become a possible route to indoor velodrome racing. There ought to be annual World Championship races for grass track cycling that could be staged anywhere in the world, but, for the sake of empowerment, should always be staged in the Global South countries of Africa, the Caribbean or Asia.

I remember how the men's road race at the 2022 Commonwealth Games in Birmingham gave a clear picture of how white and European riders dominate the sport. From a 122 rider start list, out of the 49 DNFs, 34 were Black riders from Africa and the Caribbean, including the entire teams from Zambia, Ghana, Botswana, Antigua and Barbuda, and Lesotho. I remember watching this race on BBC television. At the start, in the non-race neutralised zone and beginning of the first lap, talking about the riders who were being dropped, the commentator said, 'There is more action going on at the back of the race than at the front.' Most of these were the Black riders from African and Caribbean countries. Of the 73 finishers, among the riders from African and Caribbean countries four of the five Rwandan riders finished the race. Grenada and Uganda each had one rider in the race, and both finished. Two riders of the four from Belize finished, as did one of the three from Anguilla. By comparison, all riders who started from the South African, New Zealand, Scottish and English teams finished.

The Black cyclists entering the men's road race at the Commonwealth Games in 2022 exemplified an ongoing pattern. The former Great Britain rider Mark McKay shared some of his observations with me during a period when he was working as a cycling coach for Scotland:

'In two Commonwealth Games, in 2014 and 2018, I witnessed first-hand how the Black nations struggled so much to be able to participate in the racing. It was obvious that most of these nations' bike riders were just making up numbers with inadequate preparation or inadequate kit against the World Tour level of Australia, New Zealand, Canada and our home nations, not to mention, the rest of the smaller "white" nations. The Black riders were dropped, often within the first 5 to 10 miles of racing on the road, and in track and mountain biking within just a few minutes of the start of [the] competition.'

There needs to be a serious reimagining in how smaller nations from the African continent and Caribbean islands go about representing themselves at major international cycling events, otherwise the embarrassing results will remain a perpetual feature of these races. I imagine world cycling being transformed by the self-empowerment and advancement of Black people by the emergence of a sustainable World Tour team, as a collective of leading Black riders from the African continent and the Caribbean islands. This would take as a model the West Indies cricket team, nicknamed the Windies, which was very successful in the 1970s and 1980s. The Windies brought together as one phenomenal force the best cricketers from Jamaica, Barbados, Trinidad and Tobago, Antigua and Barbuda, and Guyana. They created their own way of playing a sport that in white circles is the epitome of British colonialism, breaking the traditional mould and blowing all their opponents away. It was after suffering a humiliating 5-1 Test match series defeat to Australia in 1976 that the Windies empowered themselves with a four-man fast-paced bowling machine that included the likes of Michael Holding, Andy Roberts, Colin Croft and Joel Garner. The Windies had dynamic batters such as Viv Richards, Gordon Greenidge, Clive Lloyd and Roy Fredericks. After 1979, the Windies did not lose a Test match series for 15 years. They became champions of the world by winning the first two One Day International Cricket World Cups. Arguably the catalyst for this success was their 1976 summer tour of England. This became enflamed before the games were played. In the lead-up the South African born England Captain Tony Greig said that he intended 'to make them [the West Indies] grovel.' With South Africa at that time still imprisoned by Apartheid, Greig's words were more than enough to fuel the power of this multi-national combination of Black athletes. The Windies won that cricket Test match series 3-0.

I remember watching the television during the summer of 1984 when the Windies routed England 5-0. This was dubbed as a 'Blackwash'. The Windies came again to England in 1988 and won that series 4-0. This performance on the world stage by the Windies team symbolised the self-determination and self-liberation of Black people around the world, empowered by decolonial movements across Africa and the Black pride movement in the United States in their struggles to remove themselves from racism and white colonial oppression.

It could be useful for some of the national cycling bodies of the Caribbean islands and across the African continent to apply the Windies' approach to future team formations in future Commonwealth Games, World Cycling Championships and Olympic Games. This would be a challenge to the status quo in cycling. In fact, this is not much different to the idea in sport that England, Scotland, Wales and Northern Ireland take when unifying as Great Britain for the Olympic Games and World Championships across many sports, including in cycling. I doubt Great Britain would have been so successful in so many cycling competitions over the years if not for this fusion of cross-national power. This is the same for the Windies cricket teams of the 1970s and 1980s. Although the Windies are not officially a country, the islands and people of these are a stronger collective representation of a world region, in the same way England, Scotland, Northern Ireland and Wales are for the British Isles. The same could be done for countries such as Rwanda, Eritrea, Kenya, Tanzania and Uganda in cycling for representing East Africa as one collective force.

My vision is aspirational. I recognise the complexities by the learning I have experienced through my meeting with cycling people during my visits across Black-led cycling cultures. Many cycling federations in Africa and the leading cyclists themselves are totally influenced by the

Eurocentric narrative of the sport. Some African cyclists that I spoke with across Africa, as shared earlier on in this book, either indicated or called this out as the 'corruption' that festers in the structures of their national federations, where African advancement remains stymied and controlled by the influential European paradigm of the sport. For some African cycling federations, money taken from European interest can purchase authority to control and direct the African narrative. This neo-colonial lock means that the African context is determined by the European vision, rather than African leadership and thinking about how the natural resources, expertise and willingness that are in the people connected across the continent could help to revolutionise and transform the cycling culture; to create ownership and power in that African context that can be sustained for generations to come.

In use and application of their own imaginations, African people in cycling must decolonise the power and influence of the colonial habitus in their minds. They should combine to conceive and realise a shared sense of an African cycling utopia, unlocking this through the undiscovered potential across its nations. The enactment and sustaining of such an African cycling utopia in full effect becomes their uhuru (liberation).

Where African and Caribbean cycling nations have the odds stacked against them, and yet still decide to play the European cycling game, in future I'd like to see the best of the best cyclists from across the Caribbean racing together as one collective force. Together, I think the riders could perform better. Having this would be good for the sport of cycling. I wish to see the same for the best of the best cyclists from across Eastern Africa and the Horn of Africa: Rwanda, Uganda, Eritrea, Ethiopia, Kenya, Tanzania and Burundi racing collectively as a force of 'New Black Cyclones'.

15

One Love

After my meeting with Black cycling community leaders in New York City I visited Philadelphia to host another *Black Champions in Cycling* book talk. I arrived by train to blue skies and spring-like weather on a winter's morning and took in the sight of the multiple tall buildings that give a distinctive skyline to the city. By the afternoon the weather had changed to heavy snow, and I was blown sideways by the snowstorm as I ran my way up and down the Philadelphia Museum of Art steps made famous by Sylvester Stallone in *Rocky*, allegedly in imitation of the training runs made by the local World Heavyweight Champion, boxing legend Joe Frazier. Later that afternoon, I joined up with Ajoa Abrokwa, the Black woman cyclist and social justice activist from Philadelphia. Having followed my *Black Champions in Cycling* work on Instagram she had joined in the discussions at my New York City talk and had agreed to become my USA cycling scene guide for the next few days. She also helped facilitate my talk that would take place at the Tricycle Store in Conshohocken, a former mill town on the Schuylkill River in Montgomery County, approximately 15 miles to the northwest of Philadelphia's city centre.

I wasn't sure what to think when we arrived at the Tricycle Store. This was an old wooden mill house painted in turquoise and white, and set in what seemed to be an isolated industrial estate. I saw no trace of human existence, but we opened the wooden door; it didn't creak, and we stepped inside. I immediately encountered the quirkiness of a bike shop. There were tyres, wheels and cycling kits all over the place and bike frames hung on the walls above redundant fireplaces. The store had the cosy appeal of the café and the warmth of the old house. On the second floor was an L-shaped room where chairs were arranged in rows. All tickets had been sold and a full house was expected.

Prior to coming to Philadelphia, I'd read about the Bikin' Blazers of Philadelphia who are recognised as a seminal, Black-led cycling outfit. The group first came together in 1989, with some members originally skiing enthusiasts, who used cycling to keep themselves in condition during the summer months. Prior to and around the time of the COVID-19 world pandemic lockdown of 2020, new Black-led cycling groups from Philadelphia have emerged. In 2017 Malaku 'Prince' Mekonnen set up Team Cycling Royalty to develop a new community for Black cyclists. This, he told me, was triggered by his attendance at several Gran Fondo events across the USA and seeing himself as the only Black rider among hundreds and thousands of participants at these long-distance bike rides for recreational cyclists of all abilities. Then developing Mekonnen's concept, in 2019 KRT (Kings Rule Together) and QRT (Queens Rule Together) led by J Curran, emerged on the scene with seven riders. Team Cycling Royalty, the KRT and QRT each have their own branded cycling apparel that can be purchased online. These cycling groups are leaders of local, national and international bike rides, local youth development schemes and local cycling training camps. Members of all cycling groups would be in attendance for the book talk.

Spread the word – Philadelphia. From left to right: Lana Harsahaw,
Ajoa Abrokwa, J Curran, me, Eric Williams and Maize Wimbush.

The panel for the talk consisted of Lana Harshaw, who, with Michael
Brown, set up SOAR Foundation Racing, with the mission to promote
the cycling lifestyle to the Black youth in West Philadelphia through
'Strength, Optimism, Achievement and Respect' (SOAR); Yvette
Brown, a leader of the Major Taylor Philadelphia Cycling Club;
J Curran, who was representing the KRT and QRT; Maize Wimbush,
the USA Under-16 female road-racing champion, who had travelled
from Maryland to join us; and the veteran Philadelphia racer Eric
Williams. People began to gather, and it was clear this was a multi-
racial audience of cycling enthusiasts – Americans of African,
European and Asian origin, all together – and I could feel the power
of this community cohesion in the welcoming hugs and kisses going
around. This was an evening for discussing and celebrating Black
people's presence in the sport of cycling in the past and in the present,
and for looking towards the future with optimism.

Another triple-charged caffeine coffee shot – a Tricycle Store special
– was passed my way and from this I buzzed my way through my
contributions to the talk, before giving the floor to the panel members.
I was particularly interested in what Eric Williams thought about an

increasing ethnically diverse cycling culture across Philadelphia and the USA. He said:

'The cycling scene has changed drastically in the United States in terms of diversity. In Philadelphia I've seen an increased amount of Black and Brown people getting into cycling, and more specifically bike racing. I honestly believe that the pandemic created an opportunity for many people to connect with nature and cycling became a popular choice for many people in Philadelphia. As time went on, I noticed that many Black and Brown cyclists kept riding and began to form cycling clubs that grew tremendously in size. I connected with those local clubs and built a very good relationship with them.'

From those people who'd come just to listen, I got a sense that they agreed with Eric and then, from the audience, veteran Black cyclist Paul Winkfield shared some of his experiences of cycling and racing in and around Philadelphia in the 1960s:

'There was no Black-branded racing clubs when I started in 1960s Philly. I was recruited by several older white members of the Pennsylvania Bicycle Club. These guys would meet at a boathouse coffee shop Saturday mornings and noon Sundays, all welcome. They would be very competitive racing around the River Drive Loop. I could stay with them, sometimes getting dropped then catching up, and they found me fun to hang with. When I decided to join, I was met with open arms, but I wasn't in the circle of riders who seemed to go to certain races and get club group photos. I was not told what popular races to attend. I rode with the club's Tuesday, Thursday and Saturday rides when time permitted. Racing was on Saturdays or Sundays. College races were mostly Sundays.

'I made friends with the other two Black members and trained and travelled with them to races. There was also Lambert Cycles, a Black-owned Philadelphia shop. Mr Lambert built frames and sold Zeus bikes and components. He was a race promoter and sponsored the first Major Taylor club, early mid-70s. I didn't join, but scheduled my rides with some members, as I was busy starting a team at the

University of Pennsylvania. Even then, I was the only Black and didn't meet any other Black riders representing other colleges.

'There were many Black folks riding, but not holding racing licences. There were many Black racers living in New York and its boroughs. I really didn't meet with them unless I rode their local races, like the Spring Central Park crits or Kissena Velodrome. Information about riding and racing was not always easy to find then. Today, there's social media, Instagram, Google, but there is that digital divide among us. Nonetheless, the young folk of today are much more inclusive. This is a very nice thing!'

Paul seems to have ridden his bike where he pleased, regardless of racial differences, with Black people and as a minority Black cyclist in white circles, too. Although perhaps his Black identity and position in these white circles of the sport was closer to the inside edge than the centre, being left outside of that first-hand knowledge about upcoming events and omitted from team photo shoots reserved for white riders. However, Paul's reflections locate Black leadership and entrepreneurism in cycling to the Philadelphia cycling scene, decades ago, through Lambert Cycles who were pioneers of a seminal Major Taylor cycling club. For me, the Tricycle Store book talk event was a fascinating moment of learning through a multiplicity of Black people-centred cycling stories, with Black people leading the discussion for a multi-ethnic audience. These more experienced voices and new voices in the sport connecting through one love – cycling.

––––––

After Philadelphia, I travelled to the city of Charlotte, North Carolina, to meet another new Black-led cycling group called the Bank City Bike Club. They were hosting a weekend of cycling events to celebrate the anniversary of their founding in 2019. Ajoa told me there would be a large number of Black-led cycling clubs from across the USA attending and I 'had to see it'. The first of these rides was called Friday Night Lights and was set to begin at last light, just before dusk. I didn't know what to expect really, but when we pulled into the parking lot there were hordes of Black cyclists pulling their carbon fibre bikes and carbon fibre disc wheel rims out of the back of their vans, and off the back of their huge 4x4 trucks. There was some serious investment in the kit on show and it was exciting, because I'd never before seen Black people collectively put this sort of money into their bicycles – not in the UK or in any of the African countries where I had observed Black-led cycling culture.

It was also here that I began to see the power and influence of Major Taylor on the Black cycling community in the USA. There were cyclists representing Major Taylor Chicago, Major Taylor Los Angeles, Major Taylor Dallas, Major Taylor Louisiana, Major Taylor North Carolina, Major Taylor Oklahoma . . . Each affiliate wore their own unique Major Taylor branded jerseys, some with the printed image of the Black Cyclone, others with 1899 written in bold, the year of Taylor's World Track Sprint Championship victory. The scene gave to me how much this Black cycling community were bonded in reproducing Taylor's omnipresence.

A very large and confident group of KRT and QRT riders from Philadelphia were also present, commanding attention. Cyclists from the Level Up Cycling Movement of Miami were there, as were riders from the USA's first historically Black college or university, St Augustine's University of Raleigh, North Carolina. They had established a cycling team in April 2020 with the goal of challenging views about cycling being inaccessible or even unacceptable for Black athletes to engage with. There were also many riders kitted out in Bahati Racing kits and Justin Williams' L39ION of Los Angeles cycling jersey could not be missed. Here was a diverse array of Black cycling identities together as one huge force, something that I had never seen or experienced before in my entire cycling career.

I was aware that this event was happening in North Carolina, historically a heartland of Confederacy and white supremacism, but that was not apparent from the gathering of around 200 Black riders on this twilight evening. They were totally emancipated in what they were doing, totally empowered and oblivious to anything else outside this world of cycling that they had created for themselves. Michael Brown had driven the SOAR Foundation bus from Philadelphia to Charlotte to join the rides and had brought me a road bike to use over the weekend – I was sorted.

The mass group gathered, and we spun slowly into the heart of the city. Huge 4x4 trucks drove by us from time-to-time, blasting out Country and Western music, but I was deep in my thoughts. Here were a large group of Black cyclists, chirping away, pausing from time to time to take selfies and group photos against the backdrop of the city's distinctive skyscrapers. I rode over to the ride leader and co-founder of the event, Shaka Greene. I asked him why he and his team came up with the concept for this weekend of rides. He said:

'Like most of the newer clubs, we started during the pandemic. We were looking for a way to stay active when everything shut down. We started riding with a group of friends that we grew up with in Charlotte. It felt great to have an outlet when our normal day to day was being restricted. We were a group of men, riding bikes, Wild West-style, and we loved it! As time went on it shifted from just a fun outlet to falling in love with the sport. Mountain bikes upgraded to road bikes. T-shirts and basketball shorts upgraded to cycling kits and then to custom cycling kits. Now we use our club to get active in the communities and promote a healthy lifestyle through cycling.'

We rode by a two-storey building that was a health club with ground-to-ceiling windows overlooking the highway. I could see people inside stepping off their running and rowing machines, and rushing over to the windows to catch a glimpse of our Black mass as we rode by. Cars honked their horns as they drove by. The ride appeared to be working in attracting public attention to one aspect of the Black cycling community coming together in North Carolina and expressing their unanimous love for the bicycle.

Ajoa came by on her bike and asked me what I thought. I smiled and told her it was amazing riding with such a large group of vibrant Black cyclists. 'Well, Dr Marlon,' she responded, 'if you like this, you'd better come and see One Love in Atlanta! Everybody goes to One Love. Everyone will be there.'

———

Ajoa had planted the idea of One Love in my mind and despite spending years avoiding any sort of appetite for travelling to the

USA, I was back there again within three months for another dose of a new Black-led cycling experience. After arriving in Chicago from the UK, my connecting flight to Atlanta, Georgia, was supposed to leave at 5.30 p.m. and arrive at 7.30 p.m., but the fight from Chicago was delayed by six hours. When I did arrive at around 1.30 a.m., the airport terminal was voiceless and empty in many areas. But walking through to baggage collection speaking loudly and clearly to me was large Black and white photographic imagery across the walls of the Hartsfield–Jackson Atlanta International Airport terminal, providing me with a vivid chronology of USA civil rights history. Words and images of Black people were among their leaders, defiant in their past struggles, not for forgetting in the present.

The One Love cycling event began in 2005 and was founded by former Metro Atlanta Cycling Club president Greg Masterson, who was on a mission to promote cycling in the Black community and build camaraderie among all cyclists. Peter Tosh, Bob Marley and the Wailers' 'One Love' record was chosen by the club as the theme name for their event because of its message about uniting people. For me, given my own Jamaican parentage and growing up on a heavy diet of the music and the One Love message of reggae, I was interested to see how this translated to cycling for Black people in the USA.

Metro Atlanta Cycling Club, Georgia

The love for riding the bike had brought members of the Metro Atlanta Cycling Club together. It didn't fail to cross my mind that I would be riding with cyclists who may themselves have been involved in historic civil rights (Black Lives Matter) movements across the USA during the 1960s, if not them then their parents or grandparents. Cycling together had become their social glue for sticking together, showcasing unity and freedom through the One Love cycling event. However, their self-empowerment had not been without challenge and there was pushback from local people and the local authorities, as Metro Atlanta Cycling Club leader Glen Daniels shared with me:

'The inaugural event in 2005 drew 470 cyclists. Over the years we have had a few problems with both authorities and residents, some of it racial, some not. One year many parking tickets were issued to drivers whose cars were parked along the side of the road due to overflow. We took this to court and successfully had those citations dismissed. Although One Love is in a rural area, our routes are not closed to traffic. The majority of motorists are always patient and friendly, but there have been incidents of rude and aggressive drivers near our cycling guests. Two years ago, an armed resident threatened one of our volunteers, saying he was not allowed to direct cyclists at an intersection across from his house. Police arrived and everything ended safely. We registered about 1700 cyclists in four weeks for the 2022 event. We also know there were those in attendance that did not register, bringing the total to 1900 to 2000 attendees.'

Fortunately, there were no threatening gun-wielding residents around on the opening Friday evening of the event. On my arrival, I was automatically sucked into the One Love energy vortex. Hundreds of Black cyclists were buzzing around the place and ready to ride. Hip-hop music was blasting out of the speakers. The barbecue was smoking and jerk chicken was frying. Red, gold and green stallholders were selling cycling kits and cycling holidays to Jamaica. Hugely expensive looking bikes were being taken off the back of hugely expensive looking 4X4 vehicles that you'd find nowhere else in the world apart from in the USA. I recognised a few faces and people that I'd met from New York City, Charlotte and Philadelphia. I was told this would be huge and it was. I saw Black cyclists representing Major Taylor Cycling Club of Alabama, Major Taylor Phoenix Riders of Arizona, Major Taylor Chicago, Major Taylor Cycling Club Los Angeles, Major Taylor Cycling Club San Diego, Major Taylor East Bay, Major Taylor Cycling Club of New York/New Jersey, Major Taylor Iron Riders, Major Taylor Central Jersey, Major Taylor Cycling Clubs from New Jersey, Texas, Tennessee, Ohio, Oklahoma, Florida, Minneapolis, KRT, QRT, L39ION of Los Angeles and Bahati Racing cycling kits all around. Black Girls Do Bike cycling groups from New York and Los Angeles, Black Watts and Level Up Cycling Movement. It seemed that the entire Black cycling community of the USA had congregated to celebrate One Love.

As the ride was about to begin, I watched from a distance as all the participating cyclists were summoned to the start line by a man with a large megaphone. Before the off, the hundreds of riders stood together in silence, as if taking an oath, and then raised their fists as the man with the megaphone, who at this point was not using it, spoke to them with passion. I was unable to make out what he said, but when he finished, the hundreds of riders gave a belly-deep collective chant of 'One Love! One Love!' and then off they rode. I'd never seen anything like it. This was tribal and positively free in many senses.

Over the course of the Labor Day weekend, the One Love event had moved from one car park starting point venue to the next. It was a slick operation, all organised by the Metro Atlanta Cycling Club leadership and members. Paper maps with details of the routes were handed out by volunteers and word went round about where to meet for the next day's event. This took me to my 1990s rave scene experiences in the UK when independent event organisers would hand out their flyers before, during and after the event to let you know where the next party was happening.

As the groups of riders and individuals began to return from their first outing, music from the PA system began to blast and the DJ turned up the volume. 'One Love', the anthem of unity written by Peter Tosh, Bob Marley and the Wailers, was being played in celebration of freedom to ride your bike in unity and in power with people that you identify with most.

ACKNOWLEDGEMENTS

What a ride! What journey of discovery and learning! For your support along the way and sharing your responses to my interview questions and questionnaires, and for help sourcing photographs and permissions for this book, thank you to Rahsaan Bahati, Babalola Ajisafe, Erik Saunders, Malaku Mekonnen, Lynne Tolman, Louis Moore, Red Walters, Dr Robert Child, Valentine Nzayisenga, Ajoa Abrokwa, Llori Sharpe, Sheerie Edwards, Jacob Lempe, Arnold Sibanda, Litha Mbadlisa, Amanda Namba, Mpumelelo Mtintso, Charles Kagimu, Ese Lovina Ukpeseraye, Frank Quaye, Foster Doevi, Henry Odumu, Lana Harshaw, Michael Brown, Vida Juliet Vivie, Emmanuel Antwi, Mr Sefadzi, Sule Kangangi, Adrien Niyonshuti, Aklilu Haile, Lea-Anne Moses, Sipho Mona, Luthando Kaka, Tenesie Dixon, Ibrihim Kamara, Isata Sama Mondeh, Fatima Deborah Conteh, Jean Pierre Rumashana, Benoit Munyankindi, Pascal Ndizeye Nkunduwite, Liliane Kayirebwe, François Régis Gahurayani, Samson Ndayishimiye, Buhle Mdbale, Eric Williams, Paul Winkfield, Shaka Greene, Glen Daniels, Finley Newmark, Mikel Delagrange.

Thank you to Angelo Mutangana for your skills in bringing to life my ideas for the illustrations in this book. For your support with due diligence, asking hard questions of me, pushing for more, editing, production and publication, a huge thanks to the team at Bloomsbury Sport, London.

Finally, to Audrey and Rose-Marie: 'the purpose is in the dream, and to dream is the only way.' Thank you.

Marlon Lee Moncrieffe
August 2024

REFERENCES

Online references accessed between January 2022 and July 2024

INTRODUCTION

'The cycling began in influential discourse, stating that "history" was being made right before our eyes': BBC Sport. (2022) 'Biniam Girmay: Eritrean becomes first African to win a one-day classic with Gent-Wevelgem victory'. 27 March. https://www.bbc.co.uk/sport/cycling/60894994; Decauluwé, B. (2022) 'Birniam Girmay: 'Gent-Wevelgem win is so important for me, for my team, and for African cycling'. Velo, 27 March. https://velo.outsideonline.com/road/biniam-girmay-gent-wevelgem-win-is-so-important-for-me-for-my-team-and-for-african-cycling/

'He followed his Gent-Wevelgem victory with what was described as a 'historic' 'first Black African' victory on stage 10 of the 2022 Giro d'Italia': MacLeary, J. (2022) 'Biniam Girmay becomes first black African to win grand tour stage with historic Giro d'Italia victory'. The *Telegraph*, 17 May. https://www.telegraph.co.uk/cycling/2022/05/17/live-giro-ditalia-2022-stage-10-updates-resultsvan-der-poel and Parker, I. (2022) 'Biniam Girmay becomes first Black African to win a Grand Tour stage'. The *Independent,* 17 May. https://www.independent.co.uk/sport/cycling/biniam-girmay-giro-ditalia-2022-b2081124.html

'"The first Black", "the first Black African" and "first Black Man in History to Win a Tour de France Stage" were some of the cycling media headline terms used to announce this': *Reuters* (2024) 'Girmay becomes first Black African to win a Tour de France stage'. 1 July. https://www.reuters.com/sports/cycling/eritreas-girmay-wins-tour-de-france-stage-three-2024-07-01/; Venutolo-Mantovani, M.

(2024) 'Stage 3: Biniam Girmay Becomes First Black Man in History to Win a Tour de France Stage'. *Bicycling*, 1 July. https://www.bicycling .com/tour-de-france/a61471752/biniam-girmay-wins-stage-3-tour -de-france-2024/; and *Dereham Times* (2024) 'Biniam Girmay makes history as first black African to win a Tour de France stage'. 1 July. https://www.derehamtimes.co.uk/sport/national/24423424.biniam -girmay-makes-history-first-black-african-win-tour-de-france-stage/

'I also saw similarities in "first Black" language of Girmay's representation': Moncrieffe, M. L. (2021) *Desire, Discrimination, Determination – Black Champions in Cycling*. Rapha Racing Ltd./ BlueTrain Publishing Limited.

'Derrick Bell, the late African American legal scholar conceived this term': Bell, D. (1980) Brown v. Board of Education and the Interest-Convergence Dilemma. *Harvard Law Review*, 93(3), 518–533. doi:10.2307/1340546

CHAPTER 1 – HOW FAR CAN THE BICYCLE TAKE YOU?

'They opened a discussion entitled "Whites only": *timetrailingforum.co .uk* (2009) *Whites only?*, 3 June. http://www.timetriallingforum.co.uk /index.php?/topic/33471-whites-only/&tab=comments#comment -476971

'In 2015, the sport of cycling in Britain was described by *Cycling Weekly* as being in a "golden age"': Wynn, N. (2015) 'Why right now is Britain's golden age of cycling'. *Cycling Weekly*, 4 August.

'I wrote about this in *Velonews*: Moncrieffe, M. L. (2020) 'Commentary: Reflections on the "velodrome of whiteness" at the London Olympics'. *Velonews*. 25 June. https://velo.outsideonline.com/ road/road-culture/commentary-reflections-on-the-velodrome -of-whiteness-at-the-london-olympics/ and Moncrieffe, M.L. (2020) 'Chapter 12 – The Velodrome of Whiteness.' In *Desire, Discrimination, Determination – Black Champions in Cycling*. Rapha Racing Ltd./BlueTrain Publishing Limited.

'The original television advert was voted as Britain's favourite advert in a 2006 poll': Byrne, Ciar. (2006) 'Ridley Scott's Hovis advert is voted all-time favourite'. The *Independent*. 2 May 2006. https://www

.independent.co.uk/news/media/ridley-scott-s-hovis-advert-is-voted
-alltime-favourite-6102089.html

'It was there that I announced my research project': Moncrieffe, M.L.
(2018) (Author/Creator). (2018) *Made In Britain: Uncovering the
life-histories of Black-British Champions in Cycling.* Exhibition.
Published: 10 to 20 December. https://research.brighton.ac.uk/en/
publications/made-in-britain-uncovering-the-life-histories-of-black
-british-ch-2

CHAPTER 2 – JESUS CHRIST OF THE BLACK CYCLING
COMMUNITY

'Conrad and Terry Kerber in their book discuss how Taylor was
named the "Black Cyclone"': Kerber, C. & Kerber, T. (2014)
*Major Taylor: The Inspiring Story of a Black Cyclist and the Men
Who Helped Him Achieve Worldwide Fame.* New York: Skyhorse
Publishing.

Moncrieffe, M.L. (2021) *Desire Discrimination Determination – Black
Champions in Cycling.* Rapha Racing Ltd./BlueTrain Publishing
Limited.

'for their icon to be posthumously honoured with the Congressional
Gold Medal': Nesbitt Golden, J. (2023) 'Cycling Legend Marshall
'Major' Taylor Should Get A Congressional Gold Medal, U.S. Reps
Propose'. Published 16 June. Chicago: Block Club Chicago.

'As the writer Seth Davidson puts it': Davidson, S. (2013) 'USA
Cycling's Black Eye', in *Cycling in the South Bay,* CreateSpace
Independent Publishing Platform; 1st edition.

'On this incident, the author and journalist Daniel de Visé writes':
de Visé, D. (2018) *The Comeback: Greg Lemond, the True King
of American Cycling, and a Legendary Tour de France.* Black Cat;
Illustrated edition.

'As the cycling historian Feargal McKay puts it': McKay, F. (2022)
*Mythologies: Major Taylor, Henri Desgrange and a Wheelbarrow Full
of Centimes.* Published 9 January. podiumcafe.com https://www
.podiumcafe.com/book-corner/2022/1/9/22837935/henri-desgrange
-major-taylor-tour-de-france-racism

CHAPTER 3 – BLACK SQUARES IN WHITE CIRCLES

'I wrote about this phenomenon in my book': Moncrieffe, M.L. (2021) *Desire Discrimination Determination – Black Champions in Cycling*. Rapha Racing Ltd./BlueTrain Publishing Limited.

'Take the former professional cyclist from the USA, Rahsaan Bahati, who told *Velonews*': Welch, B. (2020) Rahsaan Bahati: 'I've had to conform to get my foot in the door'. *Velonews*, 5 June.

CHAPTER 4 – WHEN TAO TOOK THE KNEE

'Before the start of the Tour de France in 2020 I wrote in *The Conversation*': Moncrieffe, M.L. (2020) 'Tour de France 2020: facing up to professional cycling's history of anti-blackness'. *The Conversation Trust* (UK), 26 August. https://theconversation.com/tour-de-france-2020-facing-up-to -professional-cyclings-history-of-anti-blackness-142092

'Despite the restrictions on sport during the pandemic, support for the anti-racism message was being communicated in popular professional sports': Grant, M. (2020) 'Christopher Jullien proud to take the knee on return to France'. *The Times*, 21 July. https://www.thetimes.co.uk /article/christopher-jullien-proud-to-take-the-knee-on-return-to -france-3mgwot8r5; Wilson, D. (2020) 'England cricket players take a knee in support of Black Lives Matter movement'. *The Mirror,* 8 July. https://www.mirror.co.uk/sport/cricket/breaking-england-cricket -players-take-22322435; Monye, U. (2020) 'This weekend has to be day one of rugby union's fight against racism'. The *Guardian,* 13 August. https://www.theguardian.com/sport/blog/2020/aug/13/this -weekend-has-to-be-day-one-of-rugby-unions-fight-against-racism= ; Haring, B. (2020) 'NBA Restarts Its Season with New Orleans Pelicans, Utah Jazz Kneeling for National Anthem'. *Deadline*, 30 July. https://deadline.com/2020/07/nba-restarts-with-both-teams-kneeling -for-national-anthem-1203000400/; Major, D. (2020) 'MLB Players Take a Knee on Opening Day to Show Black Lives Matter'. *Black Enterprise,* 24 July. https://www.blackenterprise.com/mlb-players-take -a-knee-on-opening-day-to-show-black-lives-matter

'Among the riders that took part in the anti-racist demonstration was the B&B Hotels–Vital Concept rider Kévin Reza': Wood, M. (2021)

'Kevin Reza: 2020 Tour de France's only black rider on racism and being a voice for diversity in cycling's peloton'. *Sky Sports*, 13 April. https://www.skysports.com/more-sports/cycling/news/15264 /12269181/kevin-reza-2020-tour-de-frances-only-black-rider-on -racism-and-being-a-voice-for-diversity-in-cyclings-peloton

'Reza's presence on the 2020 Tour de France peloton provided some influence in triggering their public communication of anti-racism': Whittle, J. (2020) 'Tour de France silent on Black Lives Matter, says cyclist Kevin Reza'. The *Guardian,* 17 September. https://www .theguardian.com/sport/2020/sep/17/tour-de-france-silent-on-black -lives-matter-says-cyclist-kevin-reza

'Step forward the white British cyclist Tao Geoghegan Hart of INEOS Grenadiers': Warwick, M. (2020) 'Tao Geoghegan Hart keen to improve cycling diversity as Lizzie Deignan celebrates 2020'. BBC Sport, 20 December. https://www.bbc.co.uk/sport/cycling/55367181

'Next, in February 2021, Geoghegan Hart drew further media and public attention through an Instagram post of himself': Geoghegan Hart, T. (2021) 'Tomorrow is my first race of the 2021 season'. Instagram, 18 February. https://www.instagram.com/p/CLcBLAenLTq/

'I wrote about the confusion in what I saw in an *Advancing Anti-Racism in Cycling* article': Moncrieffe, M.L. (2021) 'How do we applaud anti-racist action in cycling beyond a sense of tokenistic superficiality?' Advanci ngantiracismincycling.com, 21 January. https://www.researchgate.net /publication/350290677_How_do_we_applaud_anti-racist_action_in _cycling_beyond_a_sense_of_tokenistic_superficiality

'In October 2021 he posted on social media a photograph of him from *Rouleur* magazine': McGrath, A. (2021) 'Inside L39ion of Los Angeles: Cycling's Most Exciting Team'. *Rouleur*, 25 October. https:// www.rouleur.cc/blogs/the-rouleur-journal/this-is-l39ion

'a key difference in public amplification that I saw given to each of their messages': Whittle, J. (2021) 'Tao Geoghegan Hart: "Everything is Political. We are all in this together"'. The *Guardian,* 21 March. https://www.theguardian.com/sport/2021/mar/02/everything-is -political-tao-geoghegan-hart-exclusive

'Geoghegan Hart spoke of taking inspiration from his hero': Chochrek, E. (2021) 'Lewis Hamilton Raises Fist After Claiming Grand Prix

Win'. *Footwear News,* 12 July. https://footwearnews.com/2020/focus
/athletic-outdoor/lewis-hamilton-raises-fist-styrian-grand-prix-win
-1203022382/

'Cycling media cheerleaders also began to sing, dance and praise in their
excitement': Ballinger, A. (2021) 'Tao Geoghegan Hart takes a knee
and reveals he will sponsor a rider to improve diversity in cycling:
"What are words without actions?"' *Cycling Weekly,* 18 February. https:/
/www.cyclingweekly.com/news/racing/tao-geoghegan-hart-takes-a
-knee-and-reveals-he-will-sponsor-a-rider-to-improve-diversity-in
-cycling-491114; *Cyclingnews* (2021) 'Tao Geoghegan Hart: Everything
is political – we are all in this together'. 2 March. https://www
.cyclingnews.com/news/tao-geoghegan-hart-everything-is-political
-we-are-all-in-this-together/; Robinson, J. (2021) 'Tao Geoghegan Hart
to sponsor individual rider in battle for diversity in cycling'. *Cyclist,*
19 February. https://www.cyclist.co.uk/news/tao-geoghegan-hart-to
-sponsor-individual-rider-in-battle-for-diversity-in-cycling

'in the selection process to become Geoghegan Hart's mentee': Benson, D.
(2021) 'From on the brink to a chance at the highest level: Red Walters
on his shot at Hagens Berman Axeon'. *Cycling News,* 5 August. https://
www.cyclingnews.com/features/from-on-the-brink-to-a-chance-at
-the-highest-level-red-walters-on-his-shot-at-hagens-berman-axeon/;
Childers, C. (2021) 'Hagens Berman Axeon and Tao Geoghegan Hart
Announce 2021 Stagiaire'. *Axe on Cycling,* 5 August. https://www
.axeoncycling.com/news/2021_stagiaire

'Walters discussed the two races that he rode at World Tour level':
Donaldson, J. (2021) 'Red Walters: "I Learned More in Two Days
Alongside the World Tour Peloton Than I Have in Two Years".' *We
Love Cycling,* 20 October. https://www.welovecycling.com/wide
/2021/10/20/red-walters-i-learned-more-in-two-days-alongside-the
-world-tour-peloton-than-i-have-in-two-years/

CHAPTER 5 – 'GO BACK TO YOUR OWN COUNTRY!'

'There was an incredible racist backlash at their failures': *BBC Sport*
(2021) 'Racist abuse of England players Marcus Rashford, Jadon
Sancho & Bukayo Saka "unforgivable".' Published: 12 July. https://
www.bbc.co.uk/sport/football/57800431

'The *Independent* reported, "Within minutes of his [Saka's] shot being saved"': Jamieson, A. (2021) 'Bukayo Saka, Jadon Sancho and Marcus Rashford racially abused online after England Euro 2020 final defeat'. Published: 12 July. The *Independent*, https://www.independent.co.uk/news/uk/home-news/bukayo-saka-racist-england-sancho-rashford-b1882303.html

'The *Guardian* and *Sky News* reported how racists livestreamed themselves on Facebook': *Sky News* (2021) 'Cheshire man sentenced for racist abuse of England players Marcus Rashford, Jadon Sancho, and Bukayo Saka after Euro 2020 final'. Published: 8 September. https://news.sky.com/story/amp/cheshire-man-sentenced-for-racist-abuse-of-england-players-marcus-rashford-jadon-sancho-and-bukayo-saka-after-euro-2020-final-12402403; The *Guardian* (2021) 'Man jailed for racially abusing Rashford, Sancho and Saka after Euro 2020 final'. Published: 3 November. https://amp.theguardian.com/football/2021/nov/03/football-fan-jailed-for-racially-abusing-rashford-sancho-and-saka-after-final-euro-2020

'My Made in Britain research work': Moncrieffe, M.L. (2018) (Author/Creator). (2018) *Made In Britain: Uncovering the Life-histories of Black-British Champions in Cycling*. Exhibition. Published: 10 to 20 December. https://research.brighton.ac.uk/en/publications/made-in-britain-uncovering-the-life-histories-of-black-british-ch-2

'I should have been selected [by Great Britain] for more World Cup races': Moncrieffe, M.L. (2021) *Desire Discrimination Determination: Black Champions in Cycling*. Rapha CC, 17 August. https://www.rapha.cc/gb/en/shop/desire,-discrimination,-determination/product/ALI01XX

'She opted to go back and represent Barbados rather than racing in Great Britain colours': Davidson, T. (2022) 'Meet the track rider who ditched British Cycling for Barbados, and her parrot Nigel'. *Cycling Weekly*, 16 October. https://www.cyclingweekly.com/racing/meet-the-track-rider-who-ditched-british-cycling-for-barbados-and-her-parrot-nigel

'During stage 16 of the 2014 Tour de France, Simon MacMichael wrote': MacMichael, S. (2014) 'Michael Albasini insists he's not racist, apologises to Europcar's Kévin Réza'. *Road CC*, 24 July. https://

road.cc/content/news/124730-michael-albasini-insists-he's-not-rac
ist-apologises-europcar's-kévin-réza

'During the third stage of the Tour de Romandie in 2017, Réza was
racially abused': BBC Sport (2017) 'Team Sky: Gianni Moscon
suspended for racially abusing rival'. 1 May. https://www.bbc.co.uk/
sport/cycling/39769163

'When talking about this in *Bicycling*, Reza said:' Reza, K. (2020)
'Racism in Pro Cycling Should Be Treated Like Doping Violations'.
Bicycling. 27 July. https://www.bicycling.com/culture/a33322712/
kevin-reza-racism/

'Some commentators on social media (not Stewart) suggested that the
criticism Bouhanni received': *Cyclingnews* (2021) 'Nacer Bouhanni:
"If Jake Stewart really saw his life flash before his eyes, I'd advise him
to give up sprinting"'. 3 April. https://www.cyclingnews.com/news/
nacer-bouhanni-if-jake-stewart-really-saw-his-life-flash-before-his
-eyes-id-advise-him-to-give-up-sprinting/

'In an interview with L'Équipe TV, Bouhanni accepted his relegation':
L'Equipe (2021) 'Nacer Bouhanni « désolé » pour Jake Stewart après
son sprint dangereux sur Cholet-Pays de Loire'. 29 March. https://
www.lequipe.fr/Cyclisme-sur-route/Actualites/Nacer-bouhanni
-desole-pour-jake-stewart-apres-son-sprint-dangereux-sur-cholet
-pays-de-loire/1237332

'On his social media, he wrote': Robinson, J. (2021) 'Nacer Bouhanni
shares examples of racist abuse he's received on social media'.
Cyclist, 6 April. https://www.cyclist.co.uk/news/nacer-bouhanni
-shares-examples-of-racist-abuse-hes-received-on-social-media

'Arguably, Bouhanni's sprinting fouls were not much different to those
committed by the Slovakian rider Peter Sagan': *Cyclingnews* (2020)
'Peter Sagan: "I didn't think it was a dangerous move"'. 10 September.
https://www.cyclingnews.com/news/peter-sagan-i-didnt-think-it
-was-a-dangerous-move/

'And this was not the first time that Sagan had offended': *The Associated
Press* (2017) 'Tour de France crash: Sagan disqualified after
elbowing, injuring Cavendish' (video). 5 July. https://www.syracuse
.com/sports/2017/07/tour_de_france_crash_sagan_cavendish_video
.html

CHAPTER 6 – THE BINIAM BOOM!

'Media headlines from around the world announcing Girmay's Tour de France stage 3 victory': *Reuters* (2024) 'Girmay becomes first Black African to win a Tour de France stage'. 1 July. https://www .reuters.com/sports/cycling/eritreas-girmay-wins-tour-de-france -stage-three-2024-07-01/ ; Venutolo-Mantovani, M. (2024) 'Stage 3: Biniam Girmay Becomes First Black Man in History to Win a Tour de France Stage'. *Bicycling*, 1 July. https://www.bicycling.com/tour -de-france/a61471752/biniam-girmay-wins-stage-3-tour-de-france -2024/ ; *Dereham Times* (2024) 'Biniam Girmay makes history as first black African to win a Tour de France stage'. 1 July. https:// www.derehamtimes.co.uk/sport/national/24423424.biniam-girmay -makes-history-first-black-african-win-tour-de-france-stage/

'"The first Black" as a headline amplifies Girmay as the new revelation': Decaluwe, B. (2022) 'Biniam Girmay: "Gent-Wevelgem win is so important for me, for my team, and for African cycling"'. *Velo News*, 27 March. https://www.velonews.com/news/road/biniam -girmay-gent-wevelgem-win-is-so-important-for-me-for-my-team -and-for-african-cycling/

'this term as giving any genuine cause for Black people's awe and celebration': Moncrieffe, M.L. (2021) *Desire Discrimination Determination: Black Champions in Cycling. Rapha CC*, 17 August. https://www.rapha.cc/gb/en/shop/desire,-discrimination, -determination/product/ALI01XX

'The "first Black" label in cycling was imposed on Nicholas Dlamini of South Africa': Frattini, K. (2021) 'Dlamini to make history as first Black South African to compete at the Tour de France'. *Cycling News*, 18 June. https://www.cyclingnews.com/news/dlamini-to-make -history-as-first-black-south-african-to-compete-at-the-tour-de -france/

'the Frenchman Kévin Reza, who had ridden multiple Tours de France – announced his retirement': 'Nicholson, K. (2021) '"I can't do it any longer": Kévin Reza announces retirement'. *Cycling Tips,* 19 June. https://www.cyclingtips.com/2021/06/kevin-reza-will-retire-at-the -end-of-the-2021-season/

'This instantly reminded me of the 2019 photograph of Nicholas Dlamini at the Tour de Yorkshire': Moncrieffe, M.L. (2021) *Desire Discrimination Determination: Black Champions in Cycling. Rapha CC*, 17 August. https://www.rapha.cc/gb/en/shop/desire, -discrimination,-determination/product/ALI01XX

'Before the race he said in *Rwanda Today*': Rwanda Today (2023) 'Chris Froome goes full circle in Tour du Rwanda'. p. 5. 25 February. www.rwandatoday.africa

'After Girmay's Gent-Wevelgen victory': Benson, D. (2022) 'Hope that Biniam Girmay's Stunning Gent-Wevelgem win will open door for more Black African riders'. *Velo News*, 27 March. https://velo.outsideonline.com/news/road/hope-that-biniam-girmays-stunning-gent-wevelgem-win-will-open-door-for-more-black-african-riders

'In speaking of Girmay's Gent-Wevelgem victory': Smale, S. (2022) 'Eritrean rider Biniam Girmay becomes first sub-Saharan winner of cycling classic Gent-Wevelgem'. *ABC*, 28 March https://www.abc.net.au/news/2022-03-28/eritrean-rider-biniam-girmay-wins-gent-wevelgem/100944628

'The British cycling journalist William Fotheringham wrote on social media': Fotheringham, W. (2022) 'Wonder if we will look back at today in a few years'. *X*, 27 March. https://twitter.com/willfoth/status/1508107366889410561

'views given by white South African cycling coach Doug Ryder': Velonews (2022) 'Doug Ryder on his dream to bring Africa to the tour'. 25 January. https://www.velonews.com/news/road/qa-doug-ryder-on-his-dream-to-bring-africa-to-the-tour/

'The headline of one article on the BBC Sport website read': Warwick, M. (2023) 'Tour de France: Biniam Girmay is leading a revolution in cycling'. *BBC Sport*, 14 July. https://www.bbc.co.uk/sport/cycling/66186949

'Following his maiden victory at the 2024 Tour de France, Girmay wrote on his social media accounts': Girmay, B. (2024) 'Let me open the door' [Post]. x.com, 1 July. https://x.com/grmayebiniam/status/1807833619756372229

CHAPTER 7 – REPRESENTING THE ENTIRE HUMAN RACE OF
BLACK WOMEN

'In 2021, the Eritrean road cyclist Mosana Debesay became more
widely known': Tesfay, M. (2021) 'Mosana Debesay: First Black
African Woman Cyclist at the Olympics'. Ministry of Information
Eritrea, 17 July. https://shabait.com/2021/07/17/mosana-debesay
-first-black-african-woman-cyclist-at-the-olympics/

'Celebratory discourses given to Debesay – as "the first" African to
represent Black women at the Olympics': Malanski, D. (2019)
'Carrying the torch: A decolonial approach on the Olympic
traditions connections with the Eurocentric narrative of the
Spirit'. *Diagoras: International Academic Journal on Olympic
Studies*, 3, 113â-131. https://www.diagorasjournal.com/index.php/
diagoras/article/view/67/36

'The cyclist Ayesha McGowan of the USA was correct in describing
cycling as being possibly the whitest sport on Earth': Cary, T. (2020)
'"Is cycling the whitest sport on Earth?" – Ayesha McGowan, the
first African American women's rider'. The *Telegraph*, 26 June.
https://www.telegraph.co.uk/cycling/2020/06/26/cycling-whitest
-sport-earth-ayesha-mcgowan-first-african-american/

'One way the experience of a young Black woman from outside Europe
in their early twenties making an entry to the world stage': David,
M. (2021) 'Cyclist's 31 Inspirational Women No6: Teniel Campbell'.
Cyclist, 6 March. https://www.cyclist.co.uk/sponsored/cyclist-s-31
-inspirational-women-no6-teniel-campbell

'This makes me think of another Oscar-winning Black female actor,
Halle Berry': The *Sunday Morning Herald* (2006) 'Halle reveals
racism struggle'. 23 May. https://www.smh.com.au/entertainment/
celebrity/halle-reveals-racism-struggle-20060523-gdnlmx.html

CHAPTER 8 – VISITING VELOKHAYA

'South Africa's 2022 census showed Black people as the dominant
population group': Stats SA (2022) 'Census 2022. Statistics'
South Africa, Republic of South Africa. https://census.statssa
.gov.za/assets/documents/2022/P03014_Census_2022_Statistical
_Release.pdf

'Prior to looking at these numbers, and during the public dissemination of my research': Moncrieffe, M.L. (2018) (Author/ Creator). (2018). *Made In Britain: Uncovering the Life-histories of Black-British Champions in Cycling.* Exhibition. Published: 10 to 20 December. https://research.brighton.ac.uk/en/publications/made -in-britain-uncovering-the-life-histories-of-black-british-ch-2

'To provide a detailed understanding of living standards in South Africa': The World Bank (2022) 'Inequality In Southern Africa: An Assessment Of The Southern African Customs Union'. International Bank for Reconstruction and Development / The World Bank. Washington DC, USA. https://documents1.worldbank.org/curated/en/099125303072236903/ pdf/P1649270c02a1f06b0a3ae02e57eadd7a82.pdf

'I remember being ushered by teachers into the television room to watch the film *Cry Freedom*': *Cry Freedom* (1987) [Film] Dir. Richard Attenborough, USA: Universal Pictures.

'As the writer Geoff Waters discusses in his article': Waters, G. (2020) 'Racing in the shadows of mines: Black African cycle sport in South Africa's gold mines during the apartheid era'. *Classic Lightweights,* 17 August. https://www.classiclightweights.co.uk/lightweight_extras/ racing-in-the-shadows-of-mine-dumps-black-african-cycle-sport -on-south-africas-gold-mines-in-the-apartheid-era/

'Certainly, Dlamini was clearly concerned about the absence of Black riders in the 2022 Tour de France': Thewlis, T. (2022) 'Nicholas Dlamini: Tour de France diversity has taken a "disturbing step-back"'. *Cycling Weekly*, 6 July. https://www.cyclingweekly.com/news/nicholas -dlamini-tour-de-france-diversity-has-taken-a-disturbing-step-back

'When I visited Velokhaya, I wanted to learn as much as I could about the work that they do in their community; to share some stories from my book': Moncrieffe, M.L. (2021) *Desire Discrimination Determination: Black Champions in Cycling. Rapha CC*, 17 August. https://www.rapha.cc/gb/en/shop/desire,-discrimination, -determination/product/ALI01XX

'some of the criticisms of racial quotas to increase Black representation at national level in South African sport have come from the mouths of leading Black athletes': South African Institute of Race Relations (2023) 'South African Sport And The Vexed Issue Of Race'. https://

irr.org.za/fan/media/race-and-the-vexed-issue-of-south-african
-sport#:~:text=Consider%20this%20quote%20by%20Makhaya
,picked%20because%20of%20their%20colour.

'Some Black South African cricket and rugby players have spoken of
the "negative psychological impact" of quota selection': Dove, M.A.
(2019) 'What South Africa's top cricketers have to say about quotas'.
The Conversation, 18 November. https://theconversation.com/what
-south-africas-top-cricketers-have-to-say-about-quotas-127042

CHAPTER 9 – (DIS)GRACED IN THE RED, WHITE AND BLUE
'The comments whiffed of paternalistic European pity for the poor and
dependent African and brought to mind colonial writer Rudyard
Kipling's 1899 poem': Kipling, R. (1899) 'The White Man's Burden.'
https://www.kiplingsociety.co.uk/poem/poems_burden.htm

'According to Paul Kagame, president of the central-east African
Republic of Rwanda': Kagame, P. (2023) 'Seek African solutions to
African problems'. 27 February. https://www.gov.rw/blog-detail/18th
-national-umushyikirano-council-opens-in-kigali

'The educator, author and consultant in Socioeconomic Development
& Governance, David Himbara': Himbara, D. (2023) 'Kagame's
Latest Braggadocio On Rejecting Foreign Aid Recalls the Saying
that If You Tell a Big Lie and Keep Repeating It, People Will Believe
It'. *Medium,* 3 March. https://medium.com/@david.himbara_27884
/kagames-latest-braggadocio-on-rejecting-foreign-aid-recalls-the
-saying-that-if-you-tell-a-big-lie-572d39f91aac

'Rwanda and other African countries like Sierra Leone . . . are both
classified by the International Monetary Fund': International
Monetary Fund (IMF) (2020) 'IMF Executive Board Approves
Immediate Debt Relief for 25 Countries'. 13 April. https://www.imf
.org/en/News/Articles/2020/04/13/pr20151-imf-executive-board
-approves-immediate-debt-relief-for-25-countries

CHAPTER 10 – EUROPEAN ILLUSIONS IN AFRICAN DREAMS
'This has its origins in the formal partitioning of African territories
by European nations following the 1884-85 Berlin Conference':
Chamberlain, M.E. (2014) *The Scramble for Africa.* Routledge.

'European nations claimed that by colonising Africa they were also exporting civilisation to a continent which they regarded as backward and undeveloped.': Rodney, W. (2018) *How Europe Underdeveloped Africa*. Verso Books.

'Africa is a gold mine of talent. The most talent in the entire world sits within Africa. It's a question of extracting it': Union Cycliste Internationale (2022) 'Globe Riders: Africa gearing up for 2025 UCI Road World Championships in Rwanda'. 4 March 2022. https://www.uci.org/article/globe-riders-africa-gearing-up-for -2025-uci-road-world-championships-in/33uOYFn6vsVjs00 E6Jfwci

'In June 2022, the INEOS Group announced the opening of their cycling academy in Iten, Kenya': The INEOS Grenadiers (2022) 'Ineos To Launch New Cycling Academy In Kenya'. 22 June. https:// www.ineosgrenadiers.com/article/ineos-to-launch-new-cycling -academy-in-kenya

CHAPTER 11 – 'THEY'LL BE CROWNING WHITE KINGS AND QUEENS OF WORLD CYCLING – IN AFRICA!'

'UCI president David Lappartient said': *The Times of India* (2021) 'Rwanda confirmed as host of 2025 world cycling championships'. 24 September. https://timesofindia.indiatimes.com/sports/more -sports/cycling/rwanda-confirmed-as-host-of-2025-world-cycling -championships/articleshow/86490447.cms

'One UK cycling news commentator spoke of shock and concern at the decision made by the UCI': Amnesty International (2021) Amnesty International Report 2020/21; The State of the World's Human Rights; Rwanda 2020'. 7 April. https://www.ecoi.net/en/document /2048747.html

'Experts evaluating population loss in Rwanda have estimated that 800,000 Rwandans died': Human Rights Watch (2023) '[Rwanda Genocide 1994] Numbers'. Accessed: 29 May. https://www.hrw .org/reports/1999/rwanda/Geno1-3-04.htm#:~:text=expert%20 evaluating%20population%20loss%20in,at%20least%20one%20half %20million '. . . like the human tragedy of the massacre of 100,000 people and the "ethnic cleansing"':

Lampre, J.R. (2024) 'Bosnian War European history [1992–1995]'. *Brittanica,* 28 March. https://www.britannica.com/event/Bosnian-War

'I saw the news of Kigali hosting the 2025 UCI Road World Championships as an outstanding announcement for cycling': *The Times of India* (2021) 'Rwanda confirmed as host of 2025 world cycling championships'. 24 September. https://timesofindia.indiatimes .com/sports/more-sports/cycling/rwanda-confirmed-as-host-of-2025 -world-cycling-championships/articleshow/86490447.cms

'I saw Mr Kurtz, the ivory trader and central figure in Joseph Conrad's racist novel *Heart of Darkness*': Conrad, J. (1899) *Heart of Darkness.* Blackwood's Edinburgh Magazine.

'the qualification system for the 2024 UCI Road World Championships for elite men': Union Cycliste Internationale (UCI) (2024) Qualification System For The 2024 UCI Road World Championships, Allée Ferdi Kübler 12 1860 Aigle, Suisse. https:// assets.ctfassets.net/761l7gh5x5an/7lr5XVFhXs7GewfRt9dFij/cba ffecbaf21f2b3cbd661b7ae16e5f3/RWC_2024_Qualification_System _ENG_VDEF.pdf

'The Nations ranked 1 to 10 at the time of writing were in order': procyclingstats.com (2024) 'PCS Rankings: Nations'. Accessed 24 May 2024. https://www.procyclingstats.com/rankings/me/nations

'I shared my thoughts and perceptions about representation on the podium at Kigali 2025 during a *Eurosport* interview': Moncrieffe, M.L. (Curator/Producer), Ferguson, D. (Curator/Producer), & Flatley, H. (Curator/Producer) (2022). Eurosport – Discovery Channel. 'Dr Marlon Moncrieffe, *Desire Discrimination Determination – Black Champions in Cycling.* "I'd like to see a Black-British champion racing at the Tour de France for a British team"'. [Digital]Products https://www.eurosport.com/cycling/is-it-a-racist -sport-i-would-say-it-is-yes-marlon-moncrieffe-on-cycling-s-urgent -need-to-change_sto8865067/story.shtml

'On 31 May 2022 a press release from the UCI announced a memorandum of understanding': Association of National Olympic Committees of Africa (ANOCA) (2022) 2025 Union Cycliste Internationale (UCI) Road World Championships in Rwanda: 'Union Cycliste Internationale and Association of National Olympic

Committees of Africa join forces to develop African riders'. 31 May.
https://anoca.africa-newsroom.com/press/2025-union-cycliste
-internationale-uci-road-world-championships-in-rwanda-union
-cycliste-internationale-and-association-of-national-olympic
-committees-of-africa-join-forces-to-develop-african-riders?lang=en
'I was staying at the Hôtel des Mille Collines, which is depicted in the
2004 Hollywood film *Hotel Rwanda*': *Hotel Rwanda* (2005) [Film].
Dir Terry George, USA: MGM Distribution; Beloff, J. (2022) '*Hotel
Rwanda*: a film that proved to be a double-edged sword for Kigali'. *The
Conversation*, 7 November. https://theconversation.com/hotel-rwanda
-a-film-that-proved-to-be-a-double-edged-sword-for-kigali-192253

CHAPTER 12 – INTERNATIONALE VÉLO FORCE (VIF 2020)
'in response to the amateur, elite and professional Black racing
cyclists and riders who in my research': Moncrieffe, M.L. (2018)
(Author/Creator) *Made In Britain: Uncovering the Life-histories of
Black-British Champions in Cycling*. Exhibition. Published: 10 to 20
December. https://research.brighton.ac.uk/en/publications/made
-in-britain-uncovering-the-life-histories-of-black-british-ch-2
'During and briefly after the Black Lives Matter protests "diversity"
became a buzzword used by some national cycling bodies, for
example in the UK and the USA, and even the UCI': Union Cycliste
Internationale (UCI) (2023) 'Diversity and Inclusion'. Accessed: 28
May 2023. https://www.uci.org/diversity-and-inclusion/3o8vLG6
wbzkWlVQz1ocnXl
'In 2021, they announced their bringing together of 14 experts from a
variety of industries and backgrounds, as a Diversity and Inclusion
Advisory Group (DIAG)': British Cycling (2021) 'British Cycling
Publishes Landmark Equality, Diversity and Inclusion Strategy'.
9 July. https://www.britishcycling.org.uk/about/article/20210709
-about-bc-news-British-Cycling-publishes-landmark-equality-
-diversity-and-inclusion-strategy-0
'In comparison to British Cycling, USACycling, the national body in
the USA, were more vocal and active': USACycling (2023) 'Diversity,
Equity, and Inclusion'. https://usacycling.org/diversity-equity
-inclusion/plans-initiatives; Erickson, K. (2020) *Meet USA Cycling's*

Diversity, Equity and Inclusion Task Force. Published: 7 July. https://
  usacycling.org/article/meet-diversity-equity-inclusion-task-force
'USACycling introduced and drove forwards a range of inclusive
  initiatives, such as the Search for Speed track talent ID programme':
  Palermo, A. (2023) *New Track Talent Id Program Focusing on Los
  Angeles Communities. Endurance Sportswire,* 26 January. https://www
  .endurancesportswire.com/usa-cycling-launches-new-track-talent
  -id-program-focusing-on-los-angeles-communities/
'I take caution in this from the words of American professor, poet and
  civil rights activist Audre Lorde': Lorde, A. (2018) *The Master's Tools
  Will Never Dismantle The Master's House.* Penguin UK.

CHAPTER 13 – THE DIASPORIC TURN

'On my way home to the UK from Johannesburg, at the bookshop in
  Oliver Tambo International Airport, I noticed a book': Chasi, C.
  (2021) *Ubuntu for Warriors.* Africa World Press.
'For example, in 2022, 30 sexual abuse allegations were made against
  British Gymnastics as part of a UK investigation': Parmenter, T.
  (2022) 'British Gymnastics rocked by abuse report | "Starved, thirsty,
  body shamed and punished". *Sky Sports,* 17 June. https://www
  .skysports.com/more-sports/other-sports/news/29877/12635046/
  british-gymnastics-rocked-by-abuse-report-starved-thirsty-body
  -shamed-and-punished
'In the USA, women's soccer was accused of having "an extensive and
  widespread culture of sexual and emotional abuse"': Burns, K. (2022)
  'A damning report on sexual abuse in women's soccer is much
  bigger than the game.' MSNBC, 9 October. https://www.msnbc.com
  /opinion/msnbc-opinion/women-s-soccer-sexual-abuse-scandal
  -point-much-bigger-problem-n1299423
'In August 2023, the president of the Spanish football federation, Luis
  Rubiales, was widely criticised for kissing footballer Jenni Hermoso':
  Snape, J. & Kassim, A. (2023) 'Spanish football president's kiss
  sparks outrage after Women's World Cup final'. The *Guardian,* 21
  August. https://www.theguardian.com/football/2023/aug/21/luis
  -rubiales-kiss-outrage-spanish-football-fa-president-womens-world
  -cup-final-spain-jenni-hermoso

'Rubiales finally quit as head of Spain's football federation': Millan Lombrana, L., Orihuela, R. & Bloomberg (2023) 'Spanish soccer chief resigns after kissing female player on the lips: "What we saw was unacceptable". *Fortune*, 10 September. https://fortune.com/europe/2023/09/10/spanish-soccer-chief-luis-rubiales-resigns-after-kissing-female-player/

'Rubiales said the player had consented, but Hermoso rejected this as "categorically false"': MKT Jersey and Jenni Hermoso (2023) MKT Jersey Official Statement, 25 August 2023 @jennihermoso. Instagram. https://www.instagram.com/p/CwYQRo1Ppqi/?img_index=1

'The Philadelphia cycling groups Kings Rule Together (KRT) and Queens Rule Together (QRT) also share accounts': KRT & QRT (2023) 'KRT & QRT | Cycle Ghana 2023'. 19 September. https://www.krtcycling.com/post/krtqrtghana2023

'Bahati journeyed to Accra, Ghana, in 2023 with his charitable foundation for the Ride to New Horizons African Cycling Initiative.': Bahati Foundation (2023) 'July 20 – August 1, 2023, Bahati Foundation x Cycle Ghana'. https://www.bahatifoundation.org/events/cycle-ghana

'some of the riders told me that in December 2022 a $60 million US dollars indoor track cycling velodrome and multi-sports activity venue': Larweh, K. (2022) 'Ghana to get new cycling velodrome'. *Graphic Online*, 22 December. https://www.graphic.com.gh/sports/ghana-to-get-new-cycling-velodrome.html

'Ghana's severe debt crisis has caused it to take out 17 loans from the International Monetary Fund': International Monetary Fund (IMF) (2023) 'IMF Executive Board Approves US$3 Billion Extended Credit Facility Arrangement for Ghana'. Press Release No.23/151. 17 May. https://www.imf.org/en/News/Articles/2023/05/17/pr23151-ghana-imf-executive-board-approves-extended-credit-facility-arrangement-for-ghana

CHAPTER 14 – NEW BLACK CYCLONES

'When I looked at rider representation at the 2022 UCI World Junior Track Championships held in Tel Aviv': Union Cycliste Internationale (UCI) (2022) '2022 UCI Junior Track World

Championships'. https://www.uci.org/competition-hub/2022-uci
-junior-track-world-championships/3lggD68boxW0CmtjZeFsl3
'I remember how the men's road race at the 2022 Commonwealth
Games in Birmingham gave a clear picture of how white
and European riders dominate the sport': Velouk.net (2023)
'Commonwealth Games: Road Races 2022'. Accessed: 28 May. https://
www.velouk.net/2022/08/07/commonwealth-games-road-races/
'It was after suffering a humiliating 5-1 Test match series defeat to
Australia in 1976 that the Windies empowered themselves': Krishna,
S. (2016) *The Shades of 1976*. *The Cricket Monthly/* https://www
.thecricketmonthly.com/story/1034793/the-shades-of-1976
'the West Indies cricket team, nicknamed the Windies, which was very
successful in the 1970s and 1980s.': *Fire in Babylon* (2011) [Film]
Dir. Stevan Riley, UK: Passion Pictures.

CHAPTER 15 – ONE LOVE

'allegedly in imitation of the training runs made by the local World
Heavyweight Champion, boxing legend Joe Frazier': Dower, J.
(2008) 'Fight to the death'. The *Guardian*, 8 November https://www
.theguardian.com/film/2008/nov/08/joe-frazier-thriller-in-manila
'with some members originally skiing enthusiasts, who used cycling to
keep themselves in condition during the summer months.': BikinBlaz-
ers.org (2023) Accessed 2 February. https://bikinblazers.org/about-us
'In 2017 Malaku "Prince" Mekonnen set up Team Cycling Royalty':
Mekonnen, P. (2022) 'A Century Ride Helped Me Form a Club for
Black Cyclists'. *Bicycling*, 16 June. https://www.bicycling.com/health
-nutrition/a40291790/century-ride-black-cyclists/
'in 2019 KRT (Kings Rule Together) and QRT (Queens Rule Together)
led by J Curran, emerged on the scene with seven riders': Blades, N.
(2023) 'Curran Swint: Bringing Black Cyclists Together'. *Bicycling*, 19
December. https://www.bicycling.com/culture/a46030936/riders-of
-the-year-curran-swint/
'They had established a cycling team in April 2020': Patten, C.
(2020) 'Saint Augustine's University Launched The First HBCU
Cycling Team In The Country'. *USA Cycling*, 17 September. https://
usacycling.org/article/saint-augustines-first-hbcu-cycling-team

INDEX

ABOUT THE AUTHOR

Marlon Lee Moncrieffe is a former bike racer, a multiple British, European and World Championships medal winner for track sprint cycling. His debut cycling book, *Desire, Discrimination, Determination – Black Champions in Cycling* (2021), was longlisted for the 2021 William Hill Sports Book of the Year, and winner of the *Sunday Times* Cycling Book of the Year award in 2022.

PB
5648
7124-28